"This brief study focuses appropriately on the foundational principles that control the thought of Aquinas, showing, along with its notable strengths, the deep tensions inherent in it and its incompatibility as a whole with epistemology that would be true to the self-attesting revelation of God in Scripture. This fundamental failing is brought to light especially in his related views of natural reason as neutral and natural theology. The author's treatment warrants careful consideration by all those interested in understanding Thomas and subsequent Thomist positions."

—**Richard B. Gaffin Jr.**, Professor of Biblical and
Systematic Theology, Emeritus, Westminster
Theological Seminary

"Aquinas is a name not simply relegated to college textbooks on medieval philosophy or theology. There are schools and colleges by that name, one of which stands for magisterial Roman Catholic teaching.

"Oliphint takes a well-known name and gives it a life and historical context—which he accomplishes brilliantly, demonstrating Aquinas's premodern foundationalism, and then entering the complex world of Roman Catholic Aquinas interpretation. Having first mastered the massive primary sources and a host of competing scholarly interpretations, Oliphint in his clear writing style and with his vast knowledge of the material boils down complex issues as he draws his readers into solid conclusions.

"Had he stopped there, the work would be valuable for its penetrating analysis. But Oliphint's critique is the icing on the cake. Beyond the fact that Aquinas did not properly account for the depth of sin in non-Christian thinking, Oliphint argues compellingly that Aquinas was completely incorrect concerning the self-evident nature of the knowledge of God, was inadequate in his proofs for God's existence, and had a faulty doctrine of God.

"One piece of critique cake is Oliphint's analysis of God's simplicity, beginning with Aquinas and following through to Alvin Plantinga. Another is Oliphint's presentation of Aquinas's mishandling of important apologetic texts (such as the Areopagus address and parts of John), demonstrating that some of Aquinas's fundamental errors are still included in contemporary evangelical and Reformed commentaries.

"Scott Oliphint has spent a lifetime walking with Christ, speaking about Christ, preaching and teaching Christ, and defending Christ's name in the public arena. His books and articles have proved extremely helpful to me and to thousands of others. All of us interested in presenting Christ in his fullness rejoice at this latest contribution from Oliphint's pen, and we look forward to more."

—**Richard C. Gamble**, Professor of Systematic Theology,
    Reformed Presbyterian Theological Seminary

"Thomas Aquinas is a familiar name to students, clergy, and theologians. He towers over the history of theology. But his work is often simplistically dismissed or badly misunderstood. Regrettably, while many read about him, few read him. But that is rapidly changing: we are in the midst of a revival of serious interest in Aquinas, particularly among Reformed theologians. Historians of the Reformed tradition working in primary texts have reminded us of facts easily overlooked: that there is Thomas and there are Thomisms, that Thomisms of various kinds significantly influenced the early Reformed theological tradition, and that understanding the relationship of Thomisms to Reformed theology requires patience and nuance. In an earlier generation, Cornelius Van Til helped focus some of the most important epistemological and theological questions that we must ask of Aquinas and his legacy. Professor Oliphint has come along to help us do just that, with the result that we have an informed, succinct, and edifying entrée to one of the most important thinkers in the history of Christianity. Students of Aquinas would start their reading here with great profit."

—**Mark A. Garcia**, President and Fellow of Scripture and Theology, Greystone Theological Institute

"Thomas Aquinas epitomizes the best and the worst of medieval scholasticism. While acknowledging the Angelic Doctor's keen mind and prolific pen, Scott Oliphint exposes some serious defects in Aquinas's theological method that have significant ramifications for theology proper. In short, Thomas attempts to place sacred theology on an edifice of 'natural theology' that he erects with the tools of autonomous human reason. The result, sadly, is a theological enterprise that resembles the efforts of the tower-builders at Babel (Gen. 11:1–9): a theology from the ground up. In contrast, Oliphint commends a distinctively Reformed method of theology based on the principles of *sola Scriptura, sola gratia, sola fide,* and *solus Christus.* In so doing, he follows the pattern established at Bethel (Gen. 28:10–22): a theology from above that begins and ends with the self-revelation of the triune God. Serious students of theology should acquaint themselves with Aquinas's contributions to theology. But they should also be aware of his critical missteps. That's why Oliphint's primer on Aquinas's theological prolegomena is so important. I highly recommend it!"

—**Robert Gonzales**, Academic Dean, Reformed Baptist Seminary

"Despite the limited scope and brevity of Oliphint's discussion of Thomas Aquinas, it wonderfully contrasts how Aquinas and later Reformed theology think of the two foundations of the Christian faith: namely, knowledge and existence. This study accurately captures the central points of Aquinas's view and offers a cogent, biblical, Reformed corrective. Furthermore, this study nicely demonstrates how a Reformed corrective to Aquinas is foundational to a sound Christian theology today, especially as grounded in the glorious triune God and his revelation. I enthusiastically recommend this work for all students of theology and apologetics."

—**Stephen J. Wellum**, Professor of Christian Theology, The Southern Baptist Theological Seminary

Praise for the Great Thinkers Series

"After a long eclipse, intellectual history is back. We are becoming aware, once again, that ideas have consequences. The importance of P&R Publishing's leadership in this trend cannot be overstated. The series Great Thinkers: Critical Studies of Minds That Shape Us is a tool that I wish I had possessed when I was in college and early in my ministry. The scholars examined in this well-chosen group have shaped our minds and habits more than we know. Though succinct, each volume is rich, and displays a balance between what Christians ought to value and what they ought to reject. This is one of the happiest publishing events in a long time."

—**William Edgar**, Professor of Apologetics, Westminster Theological Seminary

"When I was beginning my studies of theology and philosophy during the 1950s and '60s, I profited enormously from P&R's Modern Thinkers Series. Here were relatively short books on important philosophers and theologians such as Nietzsche, Dewey, Van Til, Barth, and Bultmann, by scholars of Reformed conviction such as Clark, Van Riessen, Ridderbos, Polman, and Zuidema. These books did not merely summarize the work of these thinkers; they were serious critical interactions. Today,

P&R is resuming and updating the series, now called Great Thinkers. The new books, on people such as Aquinas, Hume, Nietzsche, Derrida, and Foucault, are written by scholars who are experts on these writers. As before, these books are short— around 100 pages. They set forth accurately the views of the thinkers under consideration, and they enter into constructive dialogue, governed by biblical and Reformed convictions. I look forward to the release of all the books being planned and to the good influence they will have on the next generation of philosophers and theologians."

—**John M. Frame**, Professor of Systematic Theology and Philosophy Emeritus, Reformed Theological Seminary, Orlando

Thomas
AQUINAS

GREAT THINKERS

A Series

Series Editor
Nathan D. Shannon

AVAILABLE IN THE GREAT THINKERS SERIES

Thomas Aquinas, by K. Scott Oliphint
Jacques Derrida, by Christopher Watkin
Karl Marx, by William D. Dennison

FORTHCOMING

Francis Bacon, by David C. Innes
Karl Barth, by Lane G. Tipton
Richard Dawkins, by Ransom H. Poythress
Michel Foucault, by Christopher Watkin
G. W. F. Hegel, by Shao Kai Tseng
David Hume, by James N. Anderson
Friedrich Nietzsche, by Carl R. Trueman
Karl Rahner, by Camden M. Bucey

Thomas
AQUINAS

K. Scott Oliphint

P&R
PUBLISHING
P.O. BOX 817 • PHILLIPSBURG • NEW JERSEY 08865-0817

Scripture quotations are from the ESV® Bible (*The Holy Bible, English Standard Version®*), copyright © 2001 by Crossway, a publishing ministry of Good News Publishers. Used by permission. All rights reserved.

Quotations from Richard A. Muller, *Post-Reformation Reformed Dogmatics: The Rise and Development of Reformed Orthodoxy, ca. 1520 to ca. 1725* (Grand Rapids: Baker Academic, 2003), are used by permission from Baker Academic, a division of Baker Publishing Group.

Italics within Scripture quotations indicate emphasis added.

ISBN: 978-1-62995-141-6 (pbk)
ISBN: 978-1-62995-142-3 (ePub)
ISBN: 978-1-62995-143-0 (MobI)

Printed in the United States of America

Library of Congress Cataloging-in-Publication Data

Names: Oliphint, K. Scott, 1955- author.
Title: Thomas Aquinas / K. Scott Oliphint.
Description: Phillipsburg : P&R Publishing, 2017. | Series: Great thinkers |
 Includes bibliographical references and index.
Identifiers: LCCN 2017022785| ISBN 9781629951416 (pbk.) | ISBN
 9781629951423 (epub) | ISBN 9781629951430 (mobi)
Subjects: LCSH: Thomas, Aquinas, Saint, 1225?-1274. | Philosophical theology.
 | Reformed Church--Doctrines.
Classification: LCC B765.T54 O5115 2017 | DDC 189/.4--dc23
LC record available at https://lccn.loc.gov/2017022785

To my mentor and colleague, William Edgar,
and his wife, Barbara—unconditional love, lived.

CONTENTS

SERIES INTRODUCTION

Amid the rise and fall of nations and civilizations, the influence of a few great minds has been profound. Some of these remain relatively obscure even as their thought shapes our world; others have become household names. As we engage our cultural and social contexts as ambassadors and witnesses for Christ, we must identify and test against the Word those thinkers who have so singularly formed the present age.

The Great Thinkers series is designed to meet the need for critically assessing the seminal thoughts of these thinkers. Great Thinkers hosts a colorful roster of authors analyzing primary source material against a background of historical contextual issues, and providing rich theological assessment and response from a Reformed perspective.

Each author was invited to meet a threefold goal, so that each Great Thinkers volume is, first, *academically informed*. The brevity of Great Thinkers volumes sets a premium on each author's command of the subject matter and on the secondary discussions that have shaped each thinker's influence. Our authors identify the most influential features of their thinkers' work and address them with precision and insight. Second, the series maintains a high standard of *biblical and theological faithfulness*. Each volume stands on an epistemic commitment to the "whole counsel of God" (Acts 20:27), and is thereby equipped for fruitful critical engagement. Finally, Great Thinkers texts are *accessible*, not burdened with jargon or unnecessarily difficult vocabulary. The goal is to inform and equip the reader as effectively as possible through clear writing, relevant analysis, and incisive, constructive critique. My hope is that this series will distinguish itself by striking with biblical faithfulness and the riches of Reformed tradition at the central nerves of culture, cultural history, and intellectual heritage.

Bryce Craig, president of P&R Publishing, deserves hearty thanks for his initiative and encouragement in setting the series in motion and seeing it through. Many thanks as well to P&R's director of academic development, John Hughes, who assumed, with cool efficiency, nearly every role on the production side of each volume. The Rev. Mark Moser carried much of the burden in the initial design of the series, acquisitions, and editing of the first several volumes. And the expert participation of Amanda Martin, P&R's editorial director, was essential at every turn. I have long admired P&R Publishing's commitment, steadfast now for over eighty-five years, to publishing excellent books promoting biblical understanding and cultural awareness, especially in the area of Christian apologetics. Sincere thanks to P&R, to these fine brothers and sisters, and to several others not mentioned here for the opportunity to serve as editor of the Great Thinkers series.

Nathan D. Shannon
Seoul, Korea

FOREWORD

A number of medieval theologians have gained wide respect from Reformed readers over the years: authors such as Anselm and Bernard of Clairvaux, John Wycliffe and Jan Hus. But Thomas Aquinas, who was in some ways the quintessential medieval theologian, has not been among them. Heavyset and taciturn, he was dubbed the "Dumb Ox" by his fellow Dominicans, but one of his teachers said of him, "This ox will one day fill the world with his bellowing." Aquinas began teaching at the University of Paris in 1252. Four years later, he was awarded the doctorate in theology and appointed a professor of philosophy at the university. Over the next eighteen years, he primarily sought to organize the knowledge of his day in the service of his medieval Catholic faith.

Although Aquinas was indebted to Augustine's theology of grace, which has deeply informed the Reformed tradition as well, his use of Aristotelian philosophy and his development of such Reformation bugbears as transubstantiation made Reformed thinkers generally wary of him. Moreover, the ardent opposition to the Reformation by a number of sixteenth-century Thomists such as Thomas Cajetan didn't help make Aquinas popular among the Reformers and undoubtedly provided a further reason for the Reformed tradition's suspicion of the Dominican theologian.

Yet the impact of Aquinas on such twentieth-century thinkers as G. K. Chesterton and Alasdair MacIntyre is indicative of the fact that he is undoubtedly a great theologian whose thought cannot be simply ignored. Thus the importance of this relatively slim monograph. Although Oliphint has limited this study of Thomas to a couple of areas of the medieval thinker's thought—epistemology and the existence and character of God—they are both foundational issues and thus well serve the monograph's twofold purpose: to reveal the strengths and weaknesses of the medieval theologian's reasoning and to reflect on how Reformed theology can best utilize the thought of this great thinker. All in all, this monograph is an excellent example of theological *ressourcement*.

Michael A. G. Haykin
Louisville, Kentucky

ACKNOWLEDGMENTS

I would like to thank Nate Shannon for inviting me to contribute to this project. Thanks also to P&R, and especially James Scott and John Hughes, for their commitment to publishing this kind of material. Thanks also to Cameron Clausing for creating the glossary for this work. Finally, thanks to my colleague, Dr. Lane Tipton, for helpful feedback and comments on portions of this work.

1

INTRODUCTION

Anyone familiar with Thomas Aquinas and his influence will be skeptical that a work of this size can do justice to him. That skepticism is warranted. Aquinas composed more than sixty works in his relatively short lifetime. Some of those works were multivolume sets. Given the sheer volume of Thomas's output, then, we must admit at the outset that the goal of this book will have to be a modest one.[1]

There are a vast number of helpful resources from and on Aquinas that one can consult with profit. We need not detail those here; some will be referenced below. Instead, what we hope to do in the pages that follow is to focus our discussion on two specific areas of concern. These concerns, we hope to make clear, will find their home in the context of Reformed theology. That is, we will argue that there are significant aspects of Thomas's thought that either cannot be incorporated into the theology that is consistent with the emphases of the Reformation, or, if

---

1. "Thomas Aquinas" means "Thomas of Aquino," referring to his ancestral home in the county of Aquino in present-day Lazio, Italy. Scholars call him either Thomas or Aquinas, and both names will be used in this book.

incorporated, must be reworked and reoriented—"reshaped," as it were—in order to be consistent with a Reformed theological context.

In order to narrow our analysis sufficiently, we will focus our attention primarily on the relationship of Aquinas's thought to the two *principia* of Reformed theology. That is, we want to analyze Thomas in light of the two foundations of the Christian faith: the foundation of *existence* (*principium essendi*), which is God himself, and the foundation of *knowledge* (*principium cognoscendi*), which is God's revelation.

In analyzing Thomas from the perspective of two central, Reformed truths, we are not promoting an anachronistic reading of him. Thomas, like all of us, was a man of his time. He did not have the advantages that we have, with two thousand years of the church's thought behind us. Thomas had only twelve hundred years of church history behind him, and thus he was not privy to the great truths that gained ascendancy from the sixteenth century forward. He did, however, have extensive and thorough knowledge of Augustine and many in the early church, as well as of Aristotle, from which the theological notion of *principium* is derived.[2] As we will demonstrate below, Thomas was well aware of the importance of a foundational starting point, both for existence and for knowledge.

Our interest, however, is not so much historical as it is theological. Though Thomas had no access to the theology that issued forth from the Reformation, he did have the same body of truth available to him in God's revelation. What he

2. According to Richard Muller, "The roots of the search for a *principium* can be extended back into the intellectual history of the Western world to Aristotle's declaration that all *archai* or first principles are the ground or 'first point from which a thing either is or comes to be or is known . . . of these some are immanent in the thing and others are outside.'" Richard A. Muller, *Post-Reformation Reformed Dogmatics: The Rise and Development of Reformed Orthodoxy, ca. 1520 to ca. 1725*, vol. 1, *Prolegomena to Theology*, 2nd ed. (Grand Rapids: Baker Academic, 2003), 431.

could not have seen historically, he could have seen biblically and theologically.

The theological analysis that we will engage in is, to be sure, much more clearly seen now. But that does not mean that we ourselves would have seen it in Thomas's day. So the point of our analysis is *not* to say that we could have seen what Thomas failed to see. Instead, it is to highlight that, as people of our own time, we should now see what Thomas did not see then, and we should be careful to expunge from our theological data those aspects of Thomas that are not consistent with the theology of Scripture, as that theology has been expressed since the Reformation.

Whatever "Reformed Thomism" might be, or might mean, in our current context, it cannot be a synthesis of biblically foreign Thomistic teachings and a consistent, biblical theology. In our theological analysis, then, we need not be historically sensitive to the neglect or near eclipse of theological accuracy. Our primary concern will be that accuracy, with less direct concern for the historical context.

Aquinas was born in southern Italy in 1224/25. When he was five or six, he was offered by his parents as an oblate to the Benedictine abbey of Monte Cassino. At the abbey, he began his study of Scripture and of the church fathers, especially Augustine and Gregory.[3]

At the age of fourteen, Thomas went to Naples to begin studies at the recently founded *studium generale*. It was there that Thomas began to study the newly translated works of Greek and Arabic philosophy.

After becoming a Dominican priest, Thomas went to Paris to study, from 1245 to 1248, under Albert the Great. There he

---

3. There are almost too many biographies of Thomas to count. The material below is a summary, primarily of the chapter "Life and Works," by Jean-Pierre Torrell, in *The Oxford Handbook of Aquinas*, ed. Brian Davies and Eleonore Stump (New York: Oxford University Press, 2012), 15–32.

was introduced to the work of Pseudo-Dionysius, as he continued as well to focus his study on the works of Aristotle. During
this time, because Thomas was a quiet and reserved student, he
earned the nickname "the Dumb Ox" (not "dumb" in intellect,
but in his lack of speech). It was Albert who, after hearing one
of Thomas's brilliant defenses, said, "We call this young man a
dumb ox, but his bellowing in doctrine will one day resound
throughout the world."[4]

After a four-year stint in Cologne (1248–52), Thomas
returned to Paris to earn his master's degree in *sacra doctrina*.
While there, Thomas worked diligently on the *Sentences* of Peter
Lombard. Lombard's *Sentences* were, in one sense, the systematic theology of the day, without which one could not presume
to be fit for theological discussion. The *Sentences* were grouped
into four books of the opinions (*sententiae*) of the church fathers
and of many medieval theologians. The four books consisted
of (1) the doctrine of God, (2) his works, (3) the incarnation,
and (4) the sacraments and last things. Thomas's comments
on the *Sentences* included around 2,000 quotes from Aristotle,
1,500 from Augustine, 500 from Denis the Areopagite, 280 from
Gregory the Great, and 240 from John Damascene, as well as
others. Clearly the influence of Aristotle on Thomas's reading
of church history was substantial and significant by this point
in his life. It was during this time that Thomas wrote *De prin-
cipiis naturae* (On the Principles of Nature) and *De ente et essentia*
(On Being and Essence). The latter work would frame his entire
metaphysical position for the rest of his life. Both of these works
"display a strong Avicennian influence."[5]

---

4. Daniel Kennedy, "St. Thomas Aquinas," in *The Catholic Encyclopedia* (New
York: Robert Appleton Company, 1912), vol. 14, http://www.newadvent.org
/cathen/14663b.htm.

5. Torrell, "Life and Works," 17. Avicenna (980–1037) has been called the first
Arabic philosopher. Through Latin translations of his work, he became a significant

It is noteworthy that Thomas, as a master of theology, composed numerous commentaries on the Bible. In addition to writing commentaries on Isaiah, Jeremiah, and Lamentations, he taught courses on Job, Matthew, John, and the Psalms. These commentaries have suffered some historical neglect, but are becoming increasingly relevant in showing the relationship between Thomas's understanding of Scripture and his more speculative theology. As we will see below, his understanding of Scripture was, in significant ways, overshadowed by his speculative thinking.

In order to understand Thomas's writing, and his entire way of thinking, it is important to recognize that, aside from writing commentaries, one of the requirements for a master of theology was to sponsor and engage in "disputed questions." After morning lessons, the master and a bachelor would join the other students in the afternoon in order to "dispute" on a given topic. Topics chosen would be discussed for three hours. The discussions would include objections, replies to the objections, and then final determinations on the question. This procedure required not simply a certain knowledge of a particular topic, but also a knowledge of the objections to the topic, replies to those objections, and the final conclusions given, all things considered. We can see why, then, Thomas's *Summa theologica* conforms to this basic approach.

During this period, Thomas wrote the only commentary in the thirteenth century on Boethius's "On the Trinity," as well as a commentary on Boethius's *De hebdomadibus*,[6] which began

---

influence on Thomas's view of being, the eternity of the world, and other topics. The best concise discussion of this can be found in John Wippel, *Metaphysical Themes in Thomas Aquinas II* (Washington, DC: Catholic University of America Press, 2014), esp. ch. 2, "The Latin Avicenna as a Source for Thomas Aquinas's Metaphysics."

6. The title is probably from Boethius's reference to "our hebdomads," or groups of seven. See Lloyd P. Gerson, ed., *The Cambridge History of Philosophy in Late Antiquity*, 2 vols. (Cambridge: Cambridge University Press, 2016), 794. Note,

Thomas's reflections on his all-important principle of participation. During this time as well, probably in 1257, Thomas (along with Bonaventure) received his doctorate of theology.

Between 1261 and 1265, Thomas wrote one of his most important works, the *Summa contra gentiles*. Torrell's assessment of this work is worth quoting:

> The work proposes to study all that human reason can discover about God:
>
> I. What is proper to God: His existence and His perfections.
>
> II. The procession of creatures from God; that is to say, the act of creation.
>
> III. The ordering of creatures to God as their end: providence and divine governance.
>
> IV. The truths inaccessible to reason and known only by faith: God as Trinity, the Incarnation of the Word and redemption, sacraments and the last things.
>
> The order of the first three books clearly echoes the structure Aquinas had already found in the *Sentences* of Lombard,

---

however: "All held that what Boethius had meant by his phrase 'from our hebdomads' was 'from axiomatic statements,' statements he could describe as such that no one who understood them could rationally deny. The formula of Boethius himself is a straight translation of the Stoic *koinai ennoiai*, 'common conceptions.' A gratuitous difficulty for his mediaeval readers was that they were faced with the mysterious term 'hebdomad,' evidently proposed by Boethius as synonymous with 'common conception'; they had no notion that 'hebdomad' means 'a seven.'" Thomas Aquinas, *An Exposition of the "On the Hebdomads" of Boethius*, trans. Janice L. Schultz and Edward A. Synan (Washington, DC: Catholic University of America Press, 2001), xxiv.

and it prefigures the circular structure that he sets out in the *Summa theologiae*: all things come from God and all things return to God under His guidance. It should also be said that this structure also follows Aquinas's own logic.[7]

It was during this time as well that Thomas developed his doctrine of the Eucharist and composed a commentary on the Gospels, the *Catena aurea*. In the *Catena*, Thomas shows remarkable familiarity with the patristic writers of the church. He is particularly fond of quoting Gregory the Great and John Chrysostom, but is most indebted to Augustine (roughly ten thousand quotations in his corpus). Thomas was also the first in the Western church to use the complete corpus of the first ecumenical councils.

By 1265, Thomas moved to Rome to found a *studium* and began in earnest to write his *Summa theologica*.[8] That work occupied him for the rest of his life, with the *Supplementum* being added by his students, who based their work on Thomas's commentary on the *Sentences*. Torrell, who gives a helpful précis of its contents, adds this:

> As to its sources, the Thomistic synthesis owes tribute to multiple philosophies from stoicism (through Cicero and St. Ambrose) to Neoplatonism (through Augustine and

7. Torrell, "Life and Works," 19.

8. We will be primarily using Thomas Aquinas, *Summa Theologica*, trans. Fathers of the English Dominican Province (Bellingham, WA: Logos Research Systems, 2009) (hereinafter *ST*). The title alternates between "*theologica*" and "*theologiae*," depending on personal preferences. Since page numbers are not given in my digital edition of the *ST*, I will cite the text location instead. Notice also: "The entire '*Summa*' contains 38 Treatises, 612 Questions, subdivided into 3120 articles, in which about 10,000 objections are proposed and answered." When Thomas stopped writing, it "had been completed only as far as the ninetieth question of the third part." Kennedy, "St. Thomas Aquinas," http://www.newadvent.org/cathen/14663b.htm.

Pseudo-Dionysius), but Aristotle is the dominant authority along with his Arabian (Avicenna and Averroës) and Jewish (Avicebron and Maimonides) commentators. From a theological point of view, the predominant influence is that of the Bible and the Fathers of the Church.[9]

Though Thomas's *Summa* is not his only important writing, it does give a useful summary of his views, some of which, however, would change as he grew older.

While in Rome, Thomas also wrote *De potentia*, a series of ten questions that deal with the power of God, but also with the relationship between God's simplicity and his triunity. During this time, Thomas also wrote a commentary on the *Divine Names*, by Pseudo-Dionysius. In this commentary, the Platonic and Neoplatonic elements of Thomas's thought are most obvious. For Thomas, however, unlike Pseudo-Dionysius, God is not beyond being, but is alone the *ipsum esse subsistens* (subsistent being itself). Thomas also wrote a number of commentaries on Aristotle's works, which commentaries were written in order to prepare for the *Summa*.

When Aquinas went back to Paris in 1268, he was engaged in controversy with many who saw Aristotle as a threat to the Christian faith. Specifically, Aristotle's view of the eternity of the world was considered to be contrary to Christian teaching. Thomas took up this matter in *De aeternitate mundi*, which was written in 1271. In this work, he endeavors to defend Aristotle, but also argues that it cannot be demonstrated that the world either is eternal or had a beginning. That matter can be settled only by faith, he says, not by reason.

By 1272, Thomas was sent back to Naples to found another *studium*. There, says Torrell, "due to repeated mystical experiences

---

9. Torrell, "Life and Works," 23.

and massive physical and nervous fatigue, Aquinas ceased writing and teaching."[10] One report of the end of Thomas's life puts it this way:

> On 6 December, 1273, he laid aside his pen and would write no more. That day he experienced an unusually long ecstasy during Mass; what was revealed to him we can only surmise from his reply to Father Reginald, who urged him to continue his writings: "I can do no more. Such secrets have been revealed to me that all I have written now appears to be of little value."[11]

On his way to the Council of Lyon, Thomas fell and died on March 7, 1274. He was canonized by John XXII in 1323, and was made a Doctor of the Church by Pius V on April 15, 1567. Nor was that all:

> In the Encyclical "Aeterni Patris", of 4 August, 1879, on the restoration of Christian philosophy, Leo XIII declared him "the prince and master of all Scholastic doctors." The same illustrious pontiff, by a Brief dated 4 August, 1880, designated him patron of all Catholic universities, academies, colleges, and schools throughout the world.[12]

As to the reasons for Thomas's genius, one author has this to say:

> Facts narrated by persons who either knew St. Thomas in life or wrote at about the time of his canonization prove that he received assistance from heaven. To Father Reginald he

10. Ibid., 27–28.
11. Kennedy, "Thomas Aquinas."
12. Ibid.

declared that he had learned more in prayer and contemplation than he had acquired from men or books. These same authors tell of mysterious visitors who came to encourage and enlighten him. The Blessed Virgin appeared, to assure him that his life and his writings were acceptable to God, and that he would persevere in his holy vocation. Sts. Peter and Paul came to aid him in interpreting an obscure passage in Isaias. When humility caused him to consider himself unworthy of the doctorate, a venerable religious of his order (supposed to be St. Dominic) appeared to encourage him and suggested the text for his opening discourse.[13]

Clearly, then, it is the view of Roman Catholic tradition that Thomas's genius was supernaturally given to him. But from a biblical, Protestant perspective, these reports have no basis in fact.

13. Ibid.

2

FOUNDATION OF KNOWLEDGE

As we seek to summarize the most significant theological teachings of Aquinas, we will set our gaze on the two foundations (*principia*) of theology: knowledge and existence. These foundations will help us properly to assess Thomas's methodology and will highlight how that methodology influences his theological content.

Although the order of these two foundations is somewhat arbitrary, we will proceed, first, to discuss the *principium cognoscendi* (foundation of knowledge) and then the *principium essendi* (foundation of existence).[1]

Reason and Revelation

At the center of Thomas's philosophical theology, from beginning to end, is his understanding and application of the

---

1. It should be noted that this is the typical order of (most) Reformed confessions. For example, the Westminster Confession of Faith begins with the doctrine of Scripture in chapter 1 and then moves to the doctrine of God in chapter 2.

relationship between that which can be gleaned by way of "natural reason" and that which is given in God's revelation. There is no debate that Thomas made this distinction, but there remains significant and often strident debate among Thomists as to the proper *structure* of this distinction. More on that below. First, however, the distinction. According to Thomas, the distinction is this:

> Now in those things which we hold about God there is truth in two ways (*duplex veritatis modus*). For certain things that are true about God wholly surpass the capability of human reason, for instance that God is three and one: while there are certain things to which even natural reason can attain, for instance that God is, that God is one, and others like these, which even the philosophers proved demonstratively of God, being guided by the light of natural reason.[2]

For Thomas, then, there is a "twofold truth of divine things."[3] The first, in methodological order, consists of all that can be known about God by natural reason, and the second consists of those divine things that can be known only by revelation. Thus:

> While then the truth of the intelligible things of God is twofold, one to which the inquiry of reason can attain, the other which surpasses the whole range of human reason, both are fittingly proposed by God to man as an object of belief.[4]

2. Thomas Aquinas, *The Summa Contra Gentiles of Saint Thomas Aquinas*, trans. the English Dominican Fathers, 5 vols. (London: Burns Oates & Washbourne, 1923–29), 1:4–5.

3. Ibid., 1:16.

4. Ibid., 1:7.

Thomas thinks that natural reason forms the foundational structure of which revelation is the superstructure, in part because of his understanding of certain biblical passages. For example, in response to his question, "Whether God Can Be Known in This Life by Natural Reason?" Thomas first quotes Romans 1:19 (in his *sed contra*),

> It is written (Rom. 1:19), *That which is known of God,* namely, what can be known of God by natural reason, *is manifest in them.*[5]

He then continues with this explanation of that passage:

> Our natural knowledge begins from sense. Hence our natural knowledge can go as far as it can be led by sensible things. But our mind cannot be led by sense so far as to see the essence of God; because the sensible effects of God do not equal the power of God as their cause. Hence from the knowledge of sensible things the whole power of God cannot be known; nor therefore can His essence be seen. But because they are His effects and depend on their cause, we can be led from them so far as to know of God *whether He exists,* and to know of Him what must necessarily belong to Him, as the first cause of all things, exceeding all things caused by Him.[6]

His understanding of Romans 1:19, then, is that the human intellect, that is, "natural reason," is able, by itself, to demonstrate the existence of God and gain some knowledge of him.

In another context, Thomas again sees the passage in Romans as referring to natural reason:

---

5. Aquinas, *ST,* I q.12 a.12 s.c.
6. Ibid., I q.12 a.12 resp. (emphasis original).

Three things lead us to believe in Christ. First of all, natural reason: "Since the creation of the world the invisible things of God are clearly known by the things that have been made" (Rom 1:20).[7]

One reason why Thomas thinks of human reason this way is found in his commentary on John 1:9 (i.e., "The true light, which gives light to everyone, was coming into the world"). In support of his view, Thomas first quotes from Theophylact:

The intellect which is given in us for our direction, and which is called natural reason, is said here to be a light given us by God.[8]

Then later he adds this:

However, if we bear in mind these distinctions and take "world" from the standpoint of its creation, and "enlighten" as referring to the light of natural reason, the statement of the Evangelist is beyond reproach. For all men coming into this visible world are enlightened by the light of natural knowledge through participating in this true light, which is the source of all the light of natural knowledge participated in by men.[9]

Thomas surmises, on the basis of these passages, that all people have and use, in identical ways, the light of natural reason, which is had by virtue of some kind of "participation" in the "true light."

---

7. Thomas Aquinas, *Commentary on the Gospel of John: Chapters 1–21*, trans. Fabian R. Larcher and James A. Weishiepl (Washington, DC: Catholic University Press of America, 2010), 241.

8. Ibid., 27.

9. Ibid., 54–55.

We should make it clear here that Thomas does not think that the "enlightening" of which John speaks necessarily includes divine truth or content. Instead, "enlightening" means that we are all able to reason in the same ways. In Thomas's construal, then, there are divine things known by natural reason, and thus available to all people, and there are divine things known by way of revelation, and thus meant only for the faithful.

We need also to mention here, though this gets little attention among Thomists, that there is a kind of knowledge mentioned by Thomas that is distinguished from these two primary kinds. Though Thomas's "twofold" knowledge is predominant in his thinking and writing, he affirms, as well, a third category:

Now there is a threefold knowledge of God. One knowledge is that by which he is known only in his effects, as if, insofar as someone knows being or something created, he has some sort of knowledge of God the creator and his creation of it, [namely an implicit knowledge]; and this knowledge is in all men naturally and from the beginning. Another knowledge is that by which God is considered in himself yet nevertheless is known through his effects, insofar as someone proceeds from the knowledge of his effects to the knowledge of God himself. And this can be had through the inquiry of natural reason, although not immediately. And it was thus that the philosophers and other wise men arrived at knowledge of God, to the extent that it is possible to attain it. The third knowledge is that by which he is known in himself and in those things that exceed all proportion to his effects. And this knowledge is neither naturally in men, nor had through the inquiry of natural reason, but had through an infused supernatural light. According to this threefold knowledge, a threefold love is found. One is that by which God is loved in his effects, insofar as when I love a creature I am said to love

God. Another love is that by which God himself is loved on the basis of his effects, and this love is had through inquiry, as when someone knowing God from his effects loves him.[10]

In this citation, Thomas affirms a kind of knowledge that all people have by virtue of being creatures in the world. This knowledge is "implicit," in that it is had neither by natural reason nor by revelation. It is a knowledge of "being" or of "happiness" (on which more is said below).

Significant as this third kind of knowledge is, it garners little to no respect in Thomas's system. The reason for its nominal status is that the content of this implicit knowledge is invariably vague and general. In the citation above, the content consists of "being [i.e., existence] or something created." In the *Summa contra gentiles*, Thomas makes this point more clearly:

> For man knows God naturally in the same way as he desires Him naturally. Now man desires Him naturally in so far as he naturally desires happiness, which is a likeness of the divine goodness. *Hence it does not follow that God considered in Himself is naturally known to man,* but that His likeness is. Wherefore man must needs come by reasoning to know God in the likenesses to Him which he discovers in God's effects.[11]

So, the first kind of this "threefold knowledge" that Thomas affirms holds little to no place in his epistemological structure. It is knowledge that shows itself in a vague and ambiguous idea, concept, or desire. The best it provides is an amorphous,

---

10. Thomas Aquinas, *On Love and Charity: Readings from the Commentary on the Sentences of Peter Lombard*, trans. Peter A. Kwasniewski, Thomas Bolin, and Joseph Bolin (Washington, DC: Catholic University of America Press, 2008), 59–60.

11. Aquinas, *Summa Contra Gentiles*, 1:21 (emphasis added).

indirect connection to who God is. For this reason, the "two-fold" knowledge of God of which Aquinas speaks is almost always highlighted by Aquinas and his followers. The first kind of knowledge, though universal and implicit, contains very little real content.

In his discussion of reason and revelation, then, we see three different kinds, or modes, of knowledge:

(1) The first is obscure and indirect, having as its objects those things which also, even if in an ambiguous and confused way, comport indirectly with aspects of God's character or of man's existence generally. This, it seems, is what Thomas means when he asserts, as quoted above, that the "true light" of which John 1:9 speaks "is the source of all the light of natural knowledge participated in by men." In other words, because we are creatures, and because we know that we and other things exist, we have a general knowledge of "being" and of the fact of creation. This is all that such an implicit knowledge can give.

(2) The second, more prominent, mode of creaturely knowledge is that which is gained through demonstration by way of our "natural reason." Here Thomas makes it clear that natural reason includes that which philosophers have employed. The fact that God's existence, and something of his character, can be proved is obvious because philosophers have shown it to be so.

(3) Third, there is knowledge that comes by revelation. This knowledge can supersede what is discerned by natural reason, but it might also include, for the faithful who are not inclined toward philosophical or demonstrative knowledge, the knowledge that can be gained by natural reason.

The Problem of Self-Evidence

The quotation presented above comes from a section in the *Summa contra gentiles* in which Thomas argues against the idea that the existence of God is self-evident to us.[12] Aquinas's notion of self-evidence and its relationship to our knowledge of God likely has its origin in Boethius. He makes a distinction between that which is self-evident *in itself*, on the one hand, and that which is self-evident *to us*, on the other.

In *Summa theologica*, Thomas asks "Whether the Existence of God is Self-Evident?"[13] After listing objections, Thomas has this to say:

> I answer that, A thing can be self-evident in either of two ways; on the one hand, self-evident in itself, though not to us; on the other, self-evident in itself, and to us. A proposition is self-evident because the predicate is included in the essence of the subject, as "Man is an animal," for animal is contained in the essence of man. *If, therefore the essence of the predicate and subject be known to all (per se nota), the proposition will be self-evident to all*; as is clear with regard to the first principles of demonstration, the terms of which are common things that no one is ignorant of, such as being and non-being, whole and part, and such like. If, however, there are some to whom the essence of the predicate and subject is unknown, the proposition will be self-evident in itself, but not to those who do not know the meaning of the predicate and subject of the proposition. Therefore, it happens, as Boëthius says (*Hebdom.*, the title of which is: "Whether all that is, is good"), "that there are some mental concepts self-evident only to the learned, as that incorporeal substances are not in space." Therefore I say that this proposition, "God exists," of itself is self-evident, for

---

12. Specifically, chapter 10 of the *Summa contra gentiles*, in book 1, is entitled, "Of the opinion of those who aver that it cannot be demonstrated that there is a God, since this is self-evident," after which, in chapter 11, Thomas moves to a "Refutation of the foregoing opinion and solution of the aforesaid arguments."

13. Aquinas, *ST*, I q.2 a.1.

the predicate is the same as the subject; because God is His own existence as will be hereafter shown (Q. III., A. 4). Now because we do not know the essence of God, the proposition is not self-evident to us; but needs to be demonstrated by things that are more known to us, though less known in their nature—namely, by effects.[14]

There are a number of aspects to this discussion that influence Thomas's response.

First, the distinction between that which is self-evident in itself (*per se*) and that which is self-evident to us is located in *propositions*. This is an extremely important point in understanding Thomas. He defines that which is self-evident by way of the relationship between a subject and a predicate in a given proposition. So, that which is self-evident *per se* is any proposition in which the predicate is, in some essential sense, contained in the subject, such as "Man is an animal," to use Thomas's example. The notion of "animal" does not exhaust that of "man," but the former is necessarily included in the latter.

A proposition, however, can be self-evident *per se* and not to us (*non est nobis per se nota*). The predicate of a proposition may in some essential way be contained in the subject, making the proposition self-evident *per se*, yet if the terms of that proposition are not known to us, then it is not self-evident to us. So, says Thomas,

> For it is simply self-evident that God is, because the selfsame thing which God is, is His existence. But since we are unable to conceive mentally the selfsame thing which is God, that thing remains unknown in regard to us.[15]

---

14. Ibid., I q.2 a.1 resp. (emphasis added).
15. Aquinas, *Summa Contra Gentiles*, 1:20.

Thomas argues that God's existence is not self-evident to us because we are not able to conceive of something in our minds to which the term "God" would apply.

Thomas also uses this occasion to refute Anselm's so-called "ontological argument."[16] In that argument, Anselm maintains that one who has the concept of "God" in his mind automatically includes in and with that concept the idea of one "than which none greater can be conceived." In other words, the content always included in the term "God," according to Anselm, is one "than which none greater can be conceived."

Thomas disagrees with Anselm. There have been those, says Thomas, who have the notion of God in mind, but who have also concluded that "this world is God."[17] Furthermore, Thomas argues that the concept of God in the mind does not necessarily guarantee that such a one exists in reality.

In response to other possible affirmations of God's subjective self-evidence, Thomas says that since God's essence cannot be known, we must come to know him through his effects. He also insists that our "natural" knowledge of God is not a knowledge of God *per se*. Instead,

> Man desires Him naturally in so far as he naturally desires happiness, which is a likeness of the divine goodness. Hence it does not follow that God considered in Himself is naturally known to man, but that His likeness is. Wherefore man must needs come by reasoning to know God in the likenesses to Him which he discovers in God's effects.[18]

16. The ascription "ontological" was Kant's, not Anselm's.

17. Aquinas, *Summa Contra Gentiles*, 1:20.

18. Ibid., 1:21. See also Aquinas, *ST*, Ia.2.1.c. Here we see again Thomas's affirmation of an implicit knowledge in man, but that knowledge is nothing but a vague notion of God's likeness, e.g., "happiness."

The existence of God, then, can in no way be self-evident to us. This point will be important as we move forward. In Thomas's epistemology, there is an unmistakable appeal to that which he considers to be general and common—the "natural"—which itself provides the foundation for anything else that we can or do know about God.

Epistemology and Metaphysics

Without providing a fuller development of Thomas's overall epistemological commitments, this might be a good place to notice a certain kind of foundationalism in Thomas's epistemological thought, but with an important codicil. Foundationalism is an epistemological structure in which certain immediate, or basic, propositions are affirmed as "foundational" to our knowledge, and then other propositions, if they are to be believed, must first be demonstrated on the basis of those immediate, or basic, propositions.

Foundationalism has been pictured, at times, as a pyramid.[19] The base of the pyramid pictures those immediate propositions that can be known apart from any demonstration. The sides of the pyramid picture those propositions that can only be known by way of demonstration from the immediate propositions known. This propositional structure comports, at least to some extent, with Thomas's view.

According to Thomas, "demonstration," by which he means syllogistic reasoning, must "proceed from principles that are immediate either straightway or through middles."[20]

19. See, for example, Ernest Sosa, "The Raft and the Pyramid: Coherence versus Foundations in the Theory of Knowledge," in *Knowledge in Perspective: Selected Essays in Epistemology*, ed. Ernest Sosa (Cambridge: Cambridge University Press, 1991), 165–91.
20. Thomas Aquinas, *Commentary on the Posterior Analytics of Aristotle*, trans.

It is necessary, therefore, for our reasoning process, that the beliefs gained thereby rest on beliefs (or knowledge) that are not inferred. In this, Thomas is classifying our beliefs as either inferred or immediate.

But there is a difference in what Thomas is saying from what many modern foundationalists want to affirm.[21] It is certainly the case that Thomas affirms propositions that are analytic; the predicate is somehow contained in the subject. Such is his meaning of immediate propositions. If propositions were in need of demonstration, they would not, therefore, be immediate. They would be mediated by way of demonstration.

Immediate propositions, then, are those in which "the predicate is included within the notion of its subject."[22] These propositions are known by virtue of themselves, and not by virtue of any inference from subject to predicate. Thus, immediate propositions are stronger than mediate ones, and are known with more certainty.

For Thomas, however, unlike contemporary foundationalism, immediate propositions are not simply *epistemic* grounds for other, mediate propositions, but, even more importantly, propositions which themselves are grounded *metaphysically*.

So, according to Scott MacDonald, "Immediate propositions, then, are capable of being known by virtue of themselves and are, therefore, proper objects of non-derivative knowledge."[23] This much could be said by virtually any foundationalist. What is more significant, however, is the following sentence: "But their actually being known by virtue of themselves *requires that one*

Fabian R. Larcher (Albany, NY: Magi Books, 1970), 17.

21. Suffice it to say at this point that, generally speaking, modern foundationalists seek to provide an epistemological structure without any reference to metaphysics.

22. Aquinas, *Commentary on the Posterior Analytics of Aristotle*, 21.

23. Scott MacDonald, "Theory of Knowledge," in *The Cambridge Companion to Aquinas*, ed. Norman Kretzmann and Eleonore Stump (Cambridge: Cambridge University Press, 1993), 172.

be acquainted with the facts expressed by those propositions which requires that one conceive the terms of those propositions."[24]

In other words, one of the key elements necessary for a proposition to be immediate is that there be a particular structure to reality. Which propositions are immediate depends on the nature of the world:

> Which propositions are immediate, then, depends solely on what real natures there are and what relations hold among them, that is, *on the basic structure of the world,* and on the psychology or belief-structure of any given epistemic subject.[25]

This emphasis marks a significant and useful difference between what Aquinas argues with respect to our beliefs and what is typically assumed in current epistemological discussions. Typically, epistemology is discussed as if it can stand on its own, without reference to, or need of, a proper understanding of reality. Not so for Thomas. For Thomas, the *nature* of that which is known is centrally important; the "pyramid" itself is in need of something on which to rest. Thus, says MacDonald,

> Propositions are immediate by virtue of expressing what might be called *metaphysically immediate relationships or facts,* the relationships that hold between natures and their essential constituents.[26]

Thomas, therefore, sees a necessary and direct link between what we believe and the nature of the world. This important addition gives our beliefs their proper epistemological ground.

---

24. Ibid. (emphasis added).
25. Ibid., 170 (emphasis added).
26. Ibid.

It recognizes that in order for there to be a justification of knowledge, a metaphysical structure must be assumed such that facts, natures and their constituents, and the relationships between them, *exist* and *are known*—and are known immediately. In other words, justification not only is epistemological, but also includes the metaphysical structure of the world. The things *known* are known by virtue of their mode of *existence*. Contrary to post-Enlightenment discussions of epistemology, in which it is thought to be separate from metaphysics, Thomas recognizes that the disciplines must be inextricably linked:

> This metaphysical picture allows us to see the kind of objectivist requirement Aquinas incorporates into the theory of demonstration. When he claims that the first principles of demonstration must be immediate and indemonstrable, he is claiming that they must express metaphysically immediate propositions and *not just propositions that are* epistemically *basic and unprovable for some particular epistemic subject.* That a given proposition *P* happens to be indemonstrable *for some person S* because there are no other propositions in *S*'s belief-structure on the basis of which *S* would be justified in holding *P* is no guarantee that *P* is, on Aquinas's view, an immediate, indemonstrable proposition. The structure of demonstration, then, is isomorphic with the metaphysical structure of reality: immediate, indemonstrable propositions express metaphysically immediate facts, whereas mediate, demonstrable propositions express metaphysically mediate facts.[27]

As we will see below, this inextricable link between epistemology and metaphysics is radically premodern; it predates the severing

27. Ibid. (emphasis added).

of epistemology and metaphysics in virtually all post-Kantian thought. More importantly, in Thomas's affirmation of the link between the two, he comes closer to a Christian understanding of epistemology and metaphysics and of the proper relation between them, than Kant and his progeny have been able to come.

Praeambula Fidei[28]

In light of all that we have seen thus far in Thomas's *principium cognoscendi*, it will be instructive for us to highlight a significant debate on the scientific structure of his epistemology.

We have already noted that, in one sense, Thomas's view is akin to a foundationalist structure, with a significant and important metaphysical codicil. Foundationalism (as well as coherentism, etc.) deals with the *propositional* structure of our knowledge. It argues that our beliefs are either propositions that are common, intuitive, and immediate, or propositions that are inferred from immediate propositions.

In the context of this debate among Thomists, however, what is in question has to do, we could say, with the *principial* structure of Thomas's epistemological proposals. The question is whether Thomas sees his philosophy as grounding theology, or theology as grounding his philosophy. In the main, the debate is between those promoting a "new" approach to Thomas and those who are intent on reclaiming and reasserting the traditional (including the traditional Roman Catholic) approach to Thomas. The traditional Roman and Thomistic view, in place for seven hundred years or so, has affirmed that *purely philosophical* "preambles of the faith" are set forth in

---

28. "Preambles of faith." These are thought, by traditional Thomists, to be philosophical principles that are necessary for the rationality of the Christian faith.

Thomas as necessary in order properly to assess the knowledge of God.[29]

Over the past sixty or so years, a new approach to Thomas has gained a significant and influential following. The new approach argues that Thomas's philosophical theology is foundationally *theological*, and not in any significant or principial way philosophical. In this new approach, one of Thomas's most prolific and influential interpreters, Cardinal Cajetan (1469–1534), is said to have been deeply and seriously mistaken in his reading of Thomas. Furthermore, the new view wants to drive a wider wedge between Thomas and Aristotle, given that the latter could not have had recourse, as Thomas did, to biblical revelation.

In his thorough and convincing argument against this new approach to Thomas, Ralph McInerny works through, in sometimes excruciating detail, the reasons and the responsible agents involved in reinterpreting Thomas's work. Leaving few stones unturned, McInerny exposes the errors of Étienne Gilson, Henri de Lubac, Marie-Dominique Chenu, and others, all of whom, in various ways, denigrate the central notion of purely philosophical "preambles of the faith" in Thomas's thinking.

McInerny's concern is that the traditional theology of the Roman Catholic church (as the proper interpreter of Aquinas) and Thomas himself contradict what the new view seeks to maintain. During the second half of the twentieth century, McInerny says, truths that were clearly set forth by Thomas have been obscured:[30]

---

29. To be clear, Thomas recognized that one could believe by faith what one is able to know by natural reason. His point is not that philosophy is *necessary* for faith, but only that what philosophy could produce by natural reason forms the rational foundation for what is believed by faith.

30. The new view has gained many of its adherents since Vatican II. Specifically, de Lubac's influence on John Paul II is unquestionable. See Andrew Dean Swafford, *Nature and Grace: A New Approach to Thomistic Ressourcement* (Eugene, OR: Pickwick Publications, 2014). Swafford hopes for a *via media* of the two views through the

Flawed understandings of the nature of Christian philosophy, a tendency to disparage the natural [i.e., philosophical] in favor of the supernatural [i.e., theological], the suggestion that the philosophy of St. Thomas is to be found only in his theological works, and cannot be separated from them . . . had the effect of weakening the notion of *praeambula fidei*.[31]

Partly at issue in the debate among Thomists is the relationship of philosophy to theology. The traditional Roman and Thomist view has been that philosophy enjoys an autonomy from theology, as it takes its place outside the realm of theology. Though philosophy is unable to grasp some of the deepest truths of theology, it can, in and of itself, grasp much truth about God and his character. The textual focus of the debate, therefore, is on the first part of the *Summa Theologica*.[32]

According to the new view, as espoused, for example, by Gilson, the only way to properly understand Thomas's view of "being" (*esse*) is in the context of revelation, specifically within the context of Exodus 3:14 (which Thomas quotes in *ST*, 1.q. 2a.3.s.c.).[33] It is this view of being, according to Gilson and others, that Cajetan confused, and thus led astray centuries of Thomistic adherents.

But McInerny's concern is that if being is *only* understood properly via revelational categories, then there is no room for that which Thomas and Thomists have taught for centuries, that

---

dogmatic theology of Matthias Scheeben.

31. Ralph McInerny, *Praeambula Fidei: Thomism and the God of the Philosophers* (Washington, DC: Catholic University of America Press, 2006), 32.

32. Speaking of this section of the *ST*, McInerny says, "This is why Thomists devote so much attention to it, and it is why theologians think they can make a name for themselves, both for genius and doctrine if, as generals attacking the enemy's strongest fortification, they bring their heaviest artillery to bear on this part of the *Summa*." Ibid., 42.

33. See ibid., 37–38 and ch. 2.

is, that philosophy is a particular and autonomous science. All that is available for a Gilsonian Thomist is a specifically *Christian* philosophy.

This, argues McInerny, only serves to suppress or misconstrue Thomas's clear teachings on the foundation for theology. With the new view, biblical revelation permeates the whole of Thomas's system. There is, then, no room in the inn for the traditional notion of natural reason in Thomas. In the new view, "natural reason" is what it is only because of a prior grace. McInerny thinks that the new view virtually destroys any place for philosophy as its own discipline.

But Thomas doesn't indicate any necessity for prior grace. He says, for example:

> The existence of God and other like truths about God, which can be known by natural reason, are not articles of faith, but are *preambles to the articles* [*non sunt articuli fidei, sed praeambula ad articulos*]; for faith presupposes natural knowledge, even as grace presupposes nature, and perfection supposes something that can be perfected.[34]

Here we see in Thomas the supposition of a "pure nature," and no idea that nature presupposes grace.

In one sense, this debate is peculiarly Romanist. It has to do with the proper place of philosophy within Roman Catholic theology. Our interest here, however, is twofold: (1) The traditional Thomist/Roman view has its roots in Thomas's affirmation of "pure nature" or "natural reason," entailing as it does the lack of the self-evidence of God's existence, as the foundation for his entire system.[35] (2) Due to the first point, the discipline of

---

34. Aquinas, *ST*, I.q.2 a.2 ad 1 (emphasis added).
35. This is the sum of McInerny's entire argument.

apologetics is rooted in the *principium* of human reason, which of itself, according to Thomas, is able to produce, by way of demonstration, a true theology.

We will discuss the matter of apologetics in a bit more detail in chapter 3. In anticipation of that, however, it is noteworthy that Thomas, while affirming that philosophy is a handmaiden to theology, nevertheless sees true theology as dependent on the truth that is gained via philosophy. Speaking of the science of theology, Thomas says:

> This science can in a sense depend upon the philosophical sciences, not as though it stood in need of them, but only in order to make its teaching clearer. For it accepts its principles not from other sciences; but immediately from God, by revelation. Therefore it does not depend upon other sciences as upon the higher, but makes use of them as of the lesser, and as handmaidens. . . .[36] That it thus uses them is not due to its own defect or insufficiency, but to the defect of our intelligence, which *is more easily led by what is known through natural reason (from which proceed the other sciences), to that which is above reason,* such as are the teachings of this science. . . . Since therefore grace does not destroy nature, but perfects it, natural reason should minister to faith as the natural bent of the will ministers to charity. Hence the Apostle says: *Bringing into captivity every understanding unto the obedience of Christ* (2 Cor. 10:5). Hence sacred doctrine makes use also of the authority of philosophers in those questions *in which they were able to know the truth by natural reason,* as Paul quotes a saying of Aratus: *As some also of your own poets said: For we are also His offspring* (Acts 17:28). Nevertheless, sacred doctrine makes use of these authorities

36. Aquinas, *ST*, I q.1 a.5 ad 2.

as extrinsic and probable arguments; but properly uses the authority of the canonical Scriptures as an incontrovertible proof. . . .[37] Hence there is no reason why those things which may be learned from philosophical science, *so far as they can be known by natural reason,* may not also be taught us by another science so far as they fall within revelation. Hence theology included in sacred doctrine differs in kind from that theology which is part of philosophy.[38]

An affirmation of the purely philosophical *praeambula fidei* allows for a reading of Thomas in which natural reason takes its proper place. If, as the new view would have it, Thomas's notion of being is strictly revelational, such that it can only be understood within the context of Exodus 3:14, then natural reason, and the self-evidence of God's existence, have no proper place to lay their heads.

It appears, then, that with respect to Thomas's *principium cognoscendi,* his realism is predominant. That realism affirms, first, the *propositional* structure of foundationalism, with certain important metaphysical qualifiers, and the *scientific* structure of theology's dependence on natural reason, that is, the science of philosophy. Those of the faithful who are not privy to philosophical discussions are nevertheless beholden to the "natural" acquisition of knowledge by way of immediate and mediate propositions.[39] Those who are involved in philosophical discussions recognize it as the foundation for that which is believed according to biblical revelation.

So far we have described Thomas's foundation of knowledge.

37. Ibid., I q.1 a.8 ad 2 (emphasis added).
38. Ibid., I q.1 a.1 ad 2 (emphases added).
39. For a more extended discussion of Thomas's realism, see K. Scott Oliphint, "Bavinck's Realism, the Logos Principle, and *Sola Scriptura,*" *Westminster Theological Journal* 72, 2 (2010): 359–90.

There is much more that can be said, but it is necessary for us now to move on to our critique.

Critique

In this section, we will address the problems inherent in Thomas's epistemology. There are a number of significant and serious issues at stake for anyone who is concerned to affirm a biblical, Reformed epistemology. We will point to the foundational errors in Thomas in order to argue for a more consistently Christian approach to the problem of knowledge.

Reason and Revelation

In thinking about the relationship of reason to revelation, there are certain general principles that everyone would affirm. It is certainly the case that we must use our reasoning and empirical faculties in order to understand the central place of biblical revelation. There is no question that people, made in the image of God, normally come into this world with the ability to think about and experience the world that God has made and in which he rules. In that sense, there is a certain temporal priority to the use of reason and our senses that is presupposed in anything else that we affirm, know, and believe.

But temporal priority does not a *principium* make. *Principia* refer, not to the *tools* that all people have and use in their commitments, but to the *content* of those commitments. They are concerned, in the first place, not with *how* their knowledge or existence originates, but with *what* that knowledge or existence *is*. It is the content of the *principia*, not the tools used in their acquisition, that is centrally important.

When we think of categories like "reason" and "revelation," then, we are not focusing on the same category. One is a tool we have and use; the other provides content for that tool. So, we want to focus, in the first place, not on the *medium* of knowledge and existence (such as the medium of reason, or of experience), but on its *content*. In that sense, *principia* are foundational in the content they contain, and that content is the foundation for everything else we know (*cognoscendi*) and are (*essendi*).

In this section of our critique, as we think about the *principium cognoscendi*, we will focus on the discussion of "Reason and Revelation" at the beginning of this chapter. That is, we will be specifically interested in Thomas's notion of natural reason.

It might be tempting to think that by "natural reason," Thomas means the reasoning faculty of the redeemed. If the new Gilsonian interpretation of Thomas were correct in its view that Thomas was exclusively concerned with theology, leaving no room for the autonomy of philosophy, then it might be the case that natural reason would have to be infused, in some way, with some kind of prevenient grace.

But this is one of the reasons why the Gilsonian view is highly suspect.[40] Thomas is clear that natural reason is that which is employed by the philosophers, especially Aristotle:

> Having shown then that it is not futile to endeavour to prove the existence of God, we may proceed to set forth the reasons whereby both philosophers and Catholic doctors have proved that there is a God. In the first place we shall give the arguments by which Aristotle sets out to prove God's existence.[41]

---

40. To be fair, there are Roman Catholic notions of grace that can be used to account for Thomas's notion of natural reason. The debate between the traditionalists and the new view has in view whether, as in the traditional account, Thomas is arguing for "pure nature" as a foundation for (the Roman Catholic notion of) the grace of redemption.

41. Aquinas, *Summa Contra Gentiles*, 1:23.

During the time of the Reformation, it became clear that this *principium* of the suitability and stability of natural reason had to be rejected. Richard Muller, whose extensive assessment of the continuities and discontinuities of Reformed theology relative to its medieval forebears is virtually without peer, has this to say about theological prolegomena in the early Reformation:

> These early Reformed statements concerning theological presuppositions focus, virtually without exception, on the problem of the knowledge of God given the fact not only of human finitude but also of human sin. The critique leveled by the Reformation at medieval theological presuppositions added a *soteriological dimension to the epistemological problem.* Whereas the medieval doctors had assumed that the fall affected primarily the will and its affections and *not the reason*, the Reformers assumed also the fallenness of the rational faculty: a generalized or "pagan" natural theology, according to the Reformers, was not merely limited to nonsaving knowledge of God—it was also bound in idolatry. This view of the problem of knowledge is the *single most important contribution of the early Reformed writers to the theological prolegomena of orthodox Protestantism.* Indeed, it is the doctrinal issue that most forcibly presses the Protestant scholastics toward the modification of the medieval models for theological prolegomena.[42]

In other words, what the medievals, including Thomas, neglected to incorporate in their theological system was the radical effect that sin has on the mind of fallen man. As Muller notes, the

---

42. Richard A. Muller, *Post-Reformation Reformed Dogmatics: The Rise and Development of Reformed Orthodoxy, ca. 1520 to ca. 1725*, vol. 1, *Prolegomena to Theology*, 2nd ed. (Grand Rapids: Baker Academic, 2003), 108 (emphasis added).

inclusion of a "soteriological dimension" in epistemological discussions is "virtually without exception" among the Reformers.
The soteriological dimension of theological prolegomena
required an antithesis between the knowledge of unbelievers and
the knowledge of Christians.

What this means is that natural reason, infected as it is,
through and through, with the ravages of sin, is wholly unable
to come to proper conclusions with respect to God and his existence. The natural knowledge of God that is demonstrated by
any and all pagan philosophies, as Muller notes, is "bound in
idolatry," in that the god it acknowledges is a god of its own imaginings, not the God of Christianity.

But what about Paul's use of the philosophers in his
Areopagus address in Acts 17? We saw above what Thomas
thinks about this. That is, "Hence sacred doctrine makes use
also of the authority of philosophers in those questions *in which
they were able to know the truth by natural reason,* as Paul quotes
a saying of Aratus: *As some also of your own poets said: For we are
also His offspring* (Acts 17:28)."

The problem with Thomas's assessment of this passage is that
he fails to appreciate the way in which Paul uses the pagan quote.
When the statement "For we also are his offspring" was first
penned by Aratus, "his" referred to Zeus. Thus, it was a statement
of idolatry. It was not, as Aquinas avers, the truth known by natural reason. It was a false statement. When the apostle Paul takes
that false statement into his own discussion, he imports into the
word "his" the biblical picture of God that he has just proclaimed
to the Athenians (Acts 17:24–27). The reference of Paul's pro-
noun "his," in other words, is completely different from Aratus's,
and that substantial difference changes a false proposition into
a true one.[43] For Paul, "his offspring" refers, not to Zeus, but to

43. For a more extended discussion of Paul at Athens, see K. Scott Oliphint,

the God whom he has just proclaimed. Thus, Paul is not referring to philosophical truth in his address on Mars Hill. Instead, he is taking an idolatrous proposition, as a point of persuasion, and transforming it into a statement of the truth about God.

The "Light" of Reason?

There is another significant point with regard to Thomas's understanding of natural reason that we must address. As we noted above, one of Thomas's central reasons for ascribing universal commonality to natural reason lies in his understanding of John 1:9. Let's quote Thomas's assessment of John 1:9 again, before we look more closely at the passage:

> However, if we bear in mind these distinctions and take "world" from the standpoint of its creation, and "enlighten" as referring to the light of natural reason, the statement of the Evangelist is beyond reproach. For all men coming into this visible world are enlightened by the light of natural knowledge through participating in this true light, which is the source of all the light of natural knowledge participated in by men.

Here Thomas was influenced by philosophical thinking, to the neglect of faithful biblical exposition. When we look closely at John 1:9 in its context, we will see that Thomas's interpretation of it has no basis in the text itself.[44]

In the prologue to his gospel, the apostle John refers, in two verses, to the Logos as "light." In verse 4, he says, "In him was life, and the life was the light of men." The question is whether the

---

Covenantal Apologetics: Principles and Practice in Defense of Our Faith (Wheaton, IL: Crossway, 2013), ch. 3.

44. We will consider briefly the prologue of John since Thomas refers to it and since it has direct application to our critical concerns.

"light" of which John speaks in this verse is the light of redemption or of creation. In view of Thomas's assessment, we also need to ask if John is referring specifically to the reasoning faculty of all people.

The clear indication of this passage is that the "light" here refers to the light that is applicable to man in God's image, that is, to every person. One reason for this is that, in the previous three verses in the prologue, John has yet to introduce the specific activity of redemption as found in Christ. His immediate concern is the cosmic and universal activity of the Logos. So, if we would paraphrase verse 4, John is telling us that the Logos gave life to man. To man as well he gives light, and he gives light to each and every person. The life that he gives to man is light, in distinction to the life that he gives to everything else. Man's life is the life of light, given by the Logos. This is probably why Thomas says that all men "participate" in the true light. However, this text has much more in view than some kind of universal "participation" in the Logos, or some amorphous reference to the "natural reason" that all people have.

The "life of light" that John introduces in verse 4 is explained more fully in verse 9. There John says, "The true light, which gives light to everyone, was coming into the world." In verse 9, John reiterates the point already made, that this Logos "was the true light" (Ἦν τὸ φῶς τὸ ἀληθινόν),[45] but he also notes that this Logos, who is the true light, was "coming into the world" (ἐρχόμενον εἰς τὸν κόσμον). In this latter phrase, the question, again, is whether John is referring to a universal cosmic activity of the Logos, as the one who was coming into the world, or whether the reference is to the Logos coming now as the incarnate Christ.

---

45. There is a question whether τὸ φῶς is the subject and ἦν . . . ἐρχόμενον the predicate, or whether the subject is supplied from the previous verses. Without rehearsing the details, we have chosen the latter, though the former is adopted by the ESV translation quoted.

The latter might seem to be the most obvious meaning, especially as John has just introduced the Baptist, who has come to announce the coming of the incarnate Logos (vv. 6–8). It seems natural to assume that the "coming into the world" in verse 9 refers to the fact that the Logos was in the process of coming as incarnate at the time of the Baptist's ministry (cf. John 11:27).

But how then shall we understand the relative clause (i.e., "which gives light to everyone"—ὃ φωτίζει πάντα ἄνθρωπον)? Is the "enlightening" (φωτίζει) of everyone by the Logos meant to be connected with the incarnate coming of the Logos, so that it is specifically redemptive, or does it refer to a more general, universal "enlightening"? And, if the latter, is it simply referring to a universal, natural reason?

We should first note, in response to this question, that the universality of John's language in this verse is beyond question. Whatever John means by "enlightening *everyone*," some account must be given of the universal application of the enlightening. It might be useful, before we offer our own account, to see how a couple of commentators have attempted to explain this passage.

Andreas Köstenberger, for example, following Raymond Brown, chooses this explanation:

> As the "true light," Jesus is here presented as the source of (spiritual) light. That light enlightens every person. . . . The present verse does not suggest universalism—the ultimate salvation of every person—for John does not speak of internal illumination in the sense of general revelation . . . but of external illumination in the sense of objective revelation requiring a response.[46]

---

46. Andreas J. Köstenberger, *John*, Baker Exegetical Commentary on the New Testament (Grand Rapids: Baker Academic, 2004), 35–36.

Köstenberger recognizes that John uses the language of a universal enlightening, but he refers it to "external illumination requiring a response," which, not being internal, does not result in salvation for all persons. For Köstenberger, what John means when he says that the Logos "gives light to everyone" is that he is the spiritual light, objectively, for everyone. He does not, however, actually *enlighten* everyone savingly. In this, Köstenberger thinks John has redemption in view.

Herman Ridderbos, in another otherwise useful commentary on John's gospel, thinks John means this in verse 9:

> Because of [Jesus'] uniqueness, it is also true of this light that it "enlightens every person" (cf. vs. 4b). This statement describes the light in its fullness and universality. It does not say that every individual is in fact enlightened by the light (cf. vss. 5, 10f.) but that by its coming into the world the light is for every human being that by which alone he or she can live (cf. 8:12).[47]

Like Köstenberger, Ridderbos sees John's use of "light" here as redemptive and objective. Instead of referring us to the universal activity of the Logos, verse 9, they both think, refers to Christ as the redemptive light of the world.

What is recognized by both of these commentators, as well, is the universality necessitated in the relative clause. There can be no question that John affirms that "everyone" (πάντα ἄνθρωπον) is *enlightened* by the true light.

What is problematic in both of these commentaries, however, is that the full force of the verb "enlightens" (φωτίζει) seems to be muted or undermined, especially if John has redemption in

---

47. Herman Ridderbos, *The Gospel of John: A Theological Commentary*, trans. John Vriend (Grand Rapids: Eerdmans, 1997), 43.

view. John does not say that the light *could* enlighten everyone, nor does he say that the light remains external to us, in some kind of objective, redemptive way. He does not say that the light *may* or *might* enlighten everyone, or even that it *will*, perhaps in the near future, enlighten everyone. Rather, he clearly affirms here that the light *enlightens* everyone.

According to Geerhardus Vos, the use of this verb "clearly passes beyond the sphere of objective potentiality into that of subjective effectuation."[48] In other words, since John says that the true light "enlightens everyone," it must be the case that everyone is, in some way, enlightened. Are we now able to affirm Thomas's notion of natural reason as taught in John's prologue?

The flow of thought in verse 9 seems to be that this Logos of whom John has spoken so majestically, who is the one who is life and light for every person, is himself, at the time of the Baptist's ministry, coming into the world. That is, the Logos is about to embark on a more specific, redemptive ministry in a way that has heretofore not been seen in the world. His "coming" is going to be a coming quite distinct from his universal presence and ministry in the world; it will be a new and different kind of "coming" into the world.

We see, then, a connection in verse 9 between the redemptive and the universal, or cosmic, aspects of the activity of the Logos. "In other words," says Vos, "the purpose of the relative clause may well be to *identify* the redemptive light with the cosmical light." Furthermore, says Vos,

> If it be objected that such a specific reference to the φωτίζειν [enlightening] to natural revelation would have to be

48. Geerhardus Vos, "The Range of the Logos Title in the Prologue to the Fourth Gospel," in *Redemptive History and Biblical Interpretation: The Shorter Writings of Geerhardus Vos*, ed. Richard B. Gaffin Jr. (Phillipsburg, NJ: Presbyterian and

indicated in some way in order to be understood, we answer, that it is sufficiently indicated by the object πάντα ἄνθρωπον [everyone]. A light of which it is said that it enlightens every man, is thereby clearly enough characterized as the general light which is common to the world as such.[49]

The most natural and obvious understanding of the relative clause, therefore, is that this true light actually, in terms of his subjective (not merely objective and potential) activity, *enlightens everyone*, even as the life which is in the Logos is the light of every person (vv. 4–5).

Thus, there is a universal, revelational activity attributed to the Logos, prior to and apart from his appearance as incarnate. Says Vos, "Here the Logos-revelation is actually mediated through the subjective life which man in dependence on the Logos possesses. The life here naturally produces the light. The meaning here is . . . that the life which man receives carries in itself and of itself kindles in him, *the light of the knowledge of God*."[50]

Here we have a direct refutation of any notion of "natural reason" that is thought to be taught in John. Instead, the universal, enlightening function of the Logos is a *revealing* function in which we all, by virtue of that activity, *know God*. We will return to this matter below. What is of supreme importance at this stage is to recognize that John 1:9, far from affirming some kind of generic light of "natural reason," as Thomas would want, instead teaches us that the cosmic activity of the Logos is his universal *revelation* of the knowledge of God that is had by all people, everywhere.

Reformed, 1980), 82. For a more extensive, nearly exhaustive, and helpful exposition of John's prologue, consult this entire article.

49. Ibid.

50. Ibid., 76 (emphasis added).

This truth takes us to a critical assessment of the notion of self-evidence as it is discussed by Aquinas.

The Problem of Self-Evidence

We will remember, from our discussion of "The Problem of Self-Evidence" earlier in this chapter, that self-evidence, for Thomas, is centrally propositional. That which is self-evident *in itself* is so because the predicate is, in some essential way, contained in the subject; Aquinas's example is "Man is an animal." A proposition that is self-evident *to us* must first be self-evident *in itself*, but it must also be the case that the terms of the proposition are known by the subject. So, the knowledge of God cannot be self-evident *to us* because, since we are "unable to conceive mentally the selfsame thing which is God, that thing remains unknown in regard to us."

Thus, also, according to Thomas, Anselm's argument for the existence of God cannot be correct because (1) many people have the word "God" in mind, but think, for example, that the world is God (so God is not the greatest conceivable being), and (2) even if they did understand "God" to mean the greatest conceivable being, the existence of such an idea in the mind is no guarantee of its existence in reality.

Furthermore, says Aquinas, what we all naturally know is not God per se. Instead, we have general and universal notions in mind—such as happiness or goodness—which themselves are only a likeness of who God is; those notions cannot be equated with knowledge of God. Universal, "implicit" knowledge is of generalities only. For true knowledge of God, he says, we must reason to his existence by way of his effects.

It may be easier to recognize the central problem in Aquinas at this point. Our brief look at John 1:9 above showed that, from the beginning of the human race, the second person of the Trinity, the Logos, has been actively revealing the knowledge of

God to each and every person. His "enlightening" activity has brought about true knowledge of God in all who are themselves the image of God.

We can support this reading of John's prologue by turning to Paul's account of general revelation in Romans 1:18–2:16. We can restrict our discussion here to verses 18–20, as those are referenced by Thomas.

As Scripture lays out the sinfulness of *all people*, both Jews and Greeks (cf. 3:9), it sets our universal rebellion against the backdrop of a universal knowledge of God:

> For the wrath of God is revealed from heaven against all ungodliness and unrighteousness of men, who by their unrighteousness suppress the truth. For what can be known about God is plain to them, because God has shown it to them. For his invisible attributes, namely, his eternal power and divine nature, have been clearly perceived, ever since the creation of the world, in the things that have been made. So they are without excuse. (Rom. 1:18–20)

Verse 18 announces the fact that God's wrath is revealed and why that wrath is revealed. The cause of God's wrath toward us is our unrighteous suppression of the truth. In other words, God's wrath is revealed from heaven because, in our wickedness and unrighteousness (in Adam), we suppress (in our souls) that which we know to be true.[51] Within the context of this general

---

51. The word translated "suppress" here is the participial form of the verb κατέχω. This verb can mean "suppress," but it can also be translated "possess" or "retain." While "suppress" is the best translation of this verb, given that the instrument of this activity is our unrighteousness, it seems likely as well that we should include, along with this suppression, the notions of retention and possession. Here there is, perhaps, a purposeful ambiguity, such that all aspects of this verb are meant to be included. Paul's own analysis of suppression will necessarily include the fact that the truth that we suppress we nevertheless continue to retain and possess. See Douglas J. Moo, *The*

announcement, however, Paul knows that he has introduced two concepts, *suppression* and *truth*, that will need clarification. In verses 19–23 (and, to some extent, verse 25), Paul develops and amplifies these two concepts.[52]

If we take verses 18–32 as a unit, we can see how Paul puts flesh on his (so far skeletal) notion of "truth" as he reiterates what he means by truth in verses 19, 20, 23, and 32 (with verse 25 repeating the notion of "the truth about God"). In each of these verses, Paul gives more specificity to the concept of truth mentioned in verse 18. We shall take these verses together in order to understand what Paul means by "the truth" that is suppressed.

In verse 19, Paul tells us that by "truth" he means "what is known about God." The truth that is suppressed, therefore, is specifically truth *about God*.[53] The way in which we come to know this truth is twofold. We come to know it, in the first place, because it is evident (φανερόν) among us.[54] Paul will expand this idea in the next verse. Before that, however, he wants us to understand just how this truth, this knowledge of God, is evident, or clear, among us.

This is vitally important for our discussion of Thomas's view of self-evidence. It is vitally important, as we will see, both

---

Epistle to the Romans, New International Commentary on the New Testament (Grand Rapids: Eerdmans, 1996), 103.

52. Verses 19 to 21 are to be seen as a part of the one declaration given in verse 18. Note the connections: διότι, v. 19; γάρ, v. 20; and διότι, v. 21.

53. As "truth," we should emphasize here, Paul is speaking of something that is known. Paul's use of γνωστός can be translated as "what is known" or "what can be known" (ESV). The former is the more common rendering, though some would see it as a redundancy when coupled with that which is clearly visible to us (cf. Moo, *Romans*, 103). It seems, however, that since Paul is concerned to explicate just what this "truth" is that we all already possess, the more common translation is more fitting. In that case, Paul is simply saying that what is (not "can be") known, is, quite literally, right before our very eyes.

54. The preposition ἐν, usually translated "in," is in verse 19 probably best translated as "among" (ESV: "to"). This does not, however, mean that there is no revelation of God in us, since God's revelation is *in* all that he has made.

because Scripture is concerned with God's activity in revealing himself (more specifically, his wrath and his other "invisible attributes"), and, in tandem with that, because Paul wants to highlight the contrast between what God is doing in this revelation, on the one hand, and what we (in Adam) do with it, on the other.

So, Paul says immediately (even before he explains the sweeping scope of that which is evident among us) that God's revelation is evident among us because *God has made it evident to us.*

We should be clear here about Scripture's emphasis. What Paul is concerned to deny, in this context, is that we, in our sins, as covenant breakers in Adam, would ever, or could ever, produce or properly infer this knowledge of God in and of ourselves. Paul wants to make sure that we are not tempted to think that the truth of God, as evident among us, is evident because *we* have marshaled the right arguments or have set our minds in the proper direction to discover it. In this, Thomas has wholly misread and misunderstood what Scripture is arguing.

The point of the argument in this entire section of Romans is to remind us of the devastating effects that sin continues to have on our minds. The truth that we know, that we retain, possess, and suppress, therefore, is truth that is, fundamentally and essentially, *given* by God to us. God is the one who ensures that this truth will get through to us. It is his action, not ours, that guarantees our possession of this truth.

The truth that we all, as creatures, know and suppress is a truth about and of God himself. It is not, as Aquinas supposes, a generic idea of happiness or goodness or being. Even more specifically (v. 20), it is a truth concerning the "invisible attributes" (τὰ ἀόρατα αὐτοῦ) of God, which Paul further specifies as his eternal power (ἀΐδιος αὐτοῦ δύναμις) and deity (θειότης).

What does Paul mean by this description? While it is perhaps not possible to be absolutely definitive, it seems that Charles Hodge is right in his assertion that what Paul has in mind here are "all the divine perfections."[55] Had Paul wanted to limit his description or to be more specific, he would more likely have delineated just exactly what characteristics of God were known through creation.

This truth that we all know, then, is the truth of God's existence, infinity, eternity, immutability, glory, wisdom, etc.[56] As Paul is developing this thought in verse 23, he speaks of this knowledge of God as "the glory of the immortal God." It is this that we all know as creatures of God. It is this that God gives, and that we necessarily receive and have as knowledge, that comes to us by virtue of God's own natural revelation (through the Logos).

There are two important aspects to this knowledge of God that are crucial to see. First, we should be clear about the context for this knowledge. It is not knowledge in the abstract of which Paul speaks. He is speaking here of a knowledge that ensues on the basis of a real relationship. It is not the kind of knowledge we might get through reading about someone or something in a book or in the newspaper. This is relational, *covenantal* knowledge. It is knowledge that comes to us because, as covenantal creatures of God, we are, always and everywhere, confronted with God himself through the things he has made. We are, even

55. Charles Hodge, *A Commentary on the Epistle to the Romans* (Grand Rapids: Louis Kregel, 1882), 37.

56. As a matter of fact, it would be difficult to improve on the Westminster Larger Catechism's description of God (Q/A 7) as an apt description of what we know by virtue of God's natural revelation: "God is a Spirit, in and of himself infinite in being, glory, blessedness, and perfection; all-sufficient, eternal, unchangeable, incomprehensible, every where present, almighty, knowing all things, most wise, most holy, most just, most merciful and gracious, long-suffering, and abundant in goodness and truth." This does not, of course, mean that every individual knows each and every one of these characteristics of God at all times. What it does mean is that they are all revealed in and through creation, to all people, throughout all of history.

as we live in God's world every day, set squarely before the face of the God who made us, and in whom we live, and move, and exist (Acts 17:28). This, then, is decidedly *personal* knowledge. It is knowledge of a person, of *the* triune, personal God, whom we have come to know by virtue of his constant and consistent revealing of himself to us.[57] This personal aspect of the knowledge of God that we have is made all the more prominent in verse 32:

> Though they know God's righteous decree that those who practice such things deserve to die, they not only do them but give approval to those who practice them.

This verse serves as a transition between Paul's exposition of God's revelation in creation in chapter 1 and of the natural revelation of God's law in chapter 2. Notice that Paul can affirm that those who are in Adam "know God's righteous decree." This knowledge of the righteous decree of God (τὸ δικαίωμα τοῦ θεοῦ) is coterminous with the knowledge of God given in natural revelation. To know God by way of natural revelation, in the way that Scripture is affirming here, is to know (at least something of) what he requires of us. Along with the knowledge of God, in other words, comes the knowledge "that those who practice such things deserve to die." Instead of repenting, however, we, in Adam, rejoice in our disobedience and attempt to gather together others who share in our rebellion. We become adept at celebrating sin and its practices.

Because this knowledge is a relational, covenantal knowledge, and because the relationship is between God and the

---

57. To be clear here, Paul does not say here that God's triunity is known through natural revelation. What he does affirm is that true knowledge of God is given by God to all human creatures.

sinner, he ensures that we all know that the violations of his law in which we willingly and happily participate are capital offenses; they place us under the penalty of death. Our knowledge of God is a responsible, covenantal knowledge that brings with it certain demands of obedience and a certain penalty of death—*and we all know it.*

Second, Paul emphasizes that this knowledge of God that we have, as given, is abundantly *clear* and *understood* (νοούμενα καθορᾶται) (v. 20). There is no obscurity in God's revelation.[58] It is not as though God masks himself in order to keep himself hidden from his human creatures.[59] The problem with the natural revelation of God—and on this we need to be as clear as possible—is not from God's side, but from ours.[60]

What we see, then, in the prologue to John's gospel and in this section in Romans, is clear and unimpeachable biblical support for the antithesis of Thomas's notion of self-evidence.

Recall from our discussion above that, at one point, Thomas notes a threefold knowledge of God. The first kind, he says, is

58. In one of his most brilliant essays, Van Til argues that the attributes that we apply to Scripture—i.e., necessity, authority, sufficiency, and perspicuity—should be applied as well to God's natural revelation. We should understand natural revelation, therefore, to be perspicuous in that the information communicated by it is never fuzzy or otherwise obscured. This, of course, does not mean that natural revelation provides a sufficient knowledge of salvation. As it was in the beginning, is now, and ever shall be, special revelation is needed for that. See Cornelius Van Til, "Nature and Scripture," in *The Infallible Word*, ed. N. B. Stonehouse and Paul Woolley (Phillipsburg, NJ: Presbyterian and Reformed, 1978).

59. Of course, God is hidden in the sense that he is incomprehensible. Most discussions of God's hiddenness in the (post?)modern philosophical context, however, center around the virtual obscurity, if not the nonexistence, of his revelation to us. See, for example, J. L. Schellenberg, *Divine Hiddenness and Human Reason* (Ithaca, NY: Cornell University Press, 1993), and Daniel Howard-Snyder and Paul K. Moser, *Divine Hiddenness: New Essays* (Cambridge: Cambridge University Press, 2002).

60. For a more detailed exegetical account of this passage, see K. Scott Oliphint, "The Irrationality of Unbelief," in *Revelation and Reason: New Essays in Reformed Apologetics*, ed. K. Scott Oliphint and Lane G. Tipton (Phillipsburg, NJ: P&R Publishing, 2007).

"that by which he is known only in his effects, as if, insofar as someone knows *being* or *something created*, he has some sort of knowledge of God the creator and his creation of it" (emphasis added). This is indeed implicit or intuitive knowledge. But for Thomas it only includes generic notions of "being" or of "something created." This kind of knowledge, for Thomas, is not true, personal, and specific knowledge of God.

Had Thomas seen the crux of Scripture's explanation of general revelation, he would have noticed that his view of self-evidence requires revisions. These revisions would include a recognition that something can be self-evident to us without requiring propositional content in our minds. Scripture is not concerned, in these passages that affirm universal knowledge of God, to specify exactly how this knowledge of God is received or held in our minds. The fact that it is the backdrop for our universal condemnation, however, requires that such knowledge not necessarily be inferred knowledge. Paul's argument is not that every person properly and intellectually processes God's natural revelation, such that we all come to the same inferential and propositional conclusions about God. As a matter of fact, the argument is that we, in our sins, whenever we do process the truth that God gives, actually suppress, deny, pollute, and pervert the clear knowledge that is given by God (the Logos) through creation. In that way, the universal knowledge of God that all have must be seen as independent of our reasoning processes. It is, we could say, our very reasoning process, as it receives the true knowledge of God given, which is grounds for our condemnation.

To put the matter another way, Scripture's point is that the existence of God is indeed self-evident, and it is self-evident *to all people, everywhere, at all times.* The reason that we don't recognize what is so obviously known by us all is not that we are not privy to a proper demonstration of God's existence. Instead, it is because we sinfully refuse to acknowledge what we know. We will not admit what we naturally acquire, as creatures made in God's image, living in the world of his exhaustive and dynamic revelation to us, in all places and at all times, from the beginning of creation into eternity future.

Epistemology and Metaphysics

With this biblical picture now in view, we can begin to see that Thomas was correct, at least formally, when he argued for the inextricable link between epistemology and metaphysics. We will remember from our discussion above that Thomas's notion of immediate knowledge and knowledge that is inferred on the basis of immediate knowledge, included, for its tenability, a particular understanding of the nature of the world. According to MacDonald, we saw that, for Thomas, "immediate, indemonstrable propositions express metaphysically immediate facts."

What we see now from Scripture is that the "metaphysically immediate facts" in the world are themselves *the revelation of God*. This revelation gets through to each and every one of us—it has been "clearly perceived, ever since the creation of the world, in the things that have been made" (Rom. 1:20). So, the normal and natural condition of man would be to acknowledge what God has unconditionally given, that is, the knowledge of his character, and to acknowledge it as something that is immediately known by us. In other words, in antithesis to Thomas's notion of self-evidence, we should recognize that, normally, the revelation of God, of which every fact consists, issues forth in our giving honor and praise to God (Rom. 1:21).

But, since the entrance of sin into the world, normal turned to abnormal. What we *ought* to do is traded for what we rebelliously *want* to do. And all we want to do, apart from redemption in Christ, is sin. Our sin causes us to suppress the truth that God gives to us through his creation.

Since, as MacDonald says of Thomas, "the structure of demonstration is isomorphic with the metaphysical structure of reality," we should see the inextricable link between the knowledge of God that comes through each and every fact of creation, and the existence of the one who has condescended to reveal himself to us. Because of this revelational activity of God, *contra* Aquinas, we do indeed have knowledge of God *intrinsically*. But our natural, sinful tendency is to work tirelessly to sever the link between the metaphysical and the epistemological. In that way, we try—in vain, to be sure—to know ourselves and our world without God. Apart from regeneration, we will never acknowledge the true God whom we all truly know.

Thomas desperately needed a closer exegetical consideration of John 1 and Romans 1. Instead, he paid closer attention to Aristotle and his Muslim followers. That attention rendered his foundations biblically untenable. He built his house of philosophical theology on sand, and no matter how ornate the rooms of such a house may be, unless they are removed from the sand and moved to the solid foundation of Scripture, they will crumble and fall.

The facts of this world are not, first of all, common and available for all to see in the same way. They are, at their core, *God's facts*, and they continue to declare the glory of God, as God is present, revealing himself in and through them all.

Praeambula Fidei

With respect to the "preambles of the faith," we can be brief in our critique. We have already noted that McInerny's argument is convincing. The traditional Roman Catholic view of Thomas, mediated as it is by Cajetan, is the only one that is able adequately to include Thomas's *principium* of "natural reason" within his philosophical theology. To argue, with the new view, that Thomas was affirming only a *Christian* philosophy, rather than a purely philosophical foundation to his theology, requires, at best, as McInerny shows, some confusing interpretations of what Thomas meant in his writings.

All told, however, it makes little difference to our critique and discussion whether the new view or the traditional view is correct. We will remember that McInerny's primary target in criticizing the new view was Étienne Gilson.

In his penetrating and pointed critique of Gilson's view of Thomism, Van Til rightly notes Gilson's problems with a notion of "being" that is derived only from reason. Reason, apart from grace, can only deal with *essences* and not with *existence*. In order to deal properly with existence, Gilson argues, one needs the light of Exodus 3:14—"I Am Who I Am." In other words, the relation of essence and existence, so central in Thomas's metaphysical system, can be properly ascertained only by revelation.

Van Til recognizes Gilson's argument, but he also sees the conundrum that such an argument presents. After quoting Gilson, Van Til says,

> Taking over this philosophy of Aristotle, St. Thomas was bound, in consequence, to "translate all the problems concerning being from the language of essences into that of existences." But could he do so without suppressing reason? Was it St. Thomas the theologian who, because of his faith, was able to make this transposition from the realm of abstract essences to that of existence? If it was, then no progress has been made in solving the problem of the relation of authority and reason. In fact the problem then seems to be more difficult than ever. For the god of Aristotle has then begun to appear to be quite different from the God of the Christian faith. Aristotle's god, it is admitted, has not created the world and does not know the world. If such a god is the natural outcome of the activity of reason when it is not enlightened by

faith does it not seem as though faith will have to reverse the decisions of reason with respect to God? A philosophy that deals with essences only would seem to resemble a merry-go-round hovering above reality but never touching it. Yet according to Rome, St. Thomas the Christian theologian need not at all ask St. Thomas the autonomous philosopher to reverse his decisions on the fundamental question about the existence of God.[61]

Here Van Til pinpoints the problem. The problem, both for the traditional view and for the new view, is that if there is a principial difference between what Aristotle was able to produce with respect to divine knowledge and what Christianity affirms about God, then how might the two *principia* be naturally and integrally related? Are they producing the same content, or is the content of one antithetical in any way to the content of the other?

According to Van Til, Gilson's new view has no way of reconciling the problem of authority and reason. It has no way adequately to synthesize what "truth" Aristotle has produced with the truth of biblical revelation. To put it another way, if it is the case that Aristotle's truth is able to deal with essences only, and not with existence, how might one merge essence and existence (as Thomas purports to do) when, as merged, one is in conflict with the other in Aristotle?

We can begin to answer this conundrum if we remember Richard Muller's assessment above. The Reformers were clear about the necessity of including the deep and dire consequences of depravity in their theological prolegomena. Once that truth is understood, applied, and developed, we begin to see that there

---

61. Cornelius Van Til, *Defense of the Faith*, 4th ed., ed. K. Scott Oliphint (Phillipsburg, NJ: P&R Publishing, 2008), 155–56.

is no such thing, since the fall, as a "natural reason" that can produce true knowledge of the true God. The best that natural reason can do, since the fall, is to produce an idol, a god of our own imaginings.

This discussion leads us naturally to an assessment of Aquinas's notion of apologetics and his proofs for the existence of God. Once we recognize what Thomas was arguing with respect to the God he purports to demonstrate, it will be necessary for us, as well, to look at Thomas's understanding of who God is.

3

FOUNDATION OF EXISTENCE

It might be helpful at this point to remember that we have a modest goal in view in this work. We hope to approach the thought of Thomas by highlighting the two foundations—the foundation of existence and the foundation of knowledge—that form the backdrop for every system of thought. In that way, we can provide an interpretive grid through which to read Thomas.

In this chapter, we want to focus on the ways in which Thomas argues for our foundation of existence, as well as the character of the one on whom our existence depends. Any Christian, including Thomas, will affirm that God alone exists in and of himself, and that he is the reason and cause of why anything else exists. Just *how* one goes about arguing for this is the crucial question here.

Our exposition and critique of Thomas will include the two aspects of Thomas's understanding of the *principium essendi*, that is, his arguments for God's existence and his assessment of who God is.

Proofs of God's Existence

Thomas's proofs of God's existence can serve as a fitting transition point between the *principium cognoscendi* and the *principium essendi*, in that they both include, and are motivated by, his notion of being (*essendi*). Being, he thinks, is understood according to "natural reason," so it is included in his natural theology (*cognoscendi*). There is, then, an overlap of Thomas's *principia* that we should recognize as we proceed to an assessment of his proofs for God's existence.

It might seem, at first glance, that the theistic proofs, as developed by Thomas Aquinas, are both too abstract and too antiquated for a post-Kantian world. Aquinas was a man intensely concerned about the science of metaphysics. He dealt, in that science, with abstractions (some would say "speculations") and methods that would never be allowed in a world subdued by the phenomenal/noumenal distinction of Immanuel Kant.

In spite of this, however, Aquinas's relevance for contemporary Christian apologetics continues to be defended and asserted. For example, in *Both/And: A Balanced Apologetic*, Ronald Mayers uses Aquinas's distinction between "intrinsic being" and "extrinsic being" in an attempt to "balance" presuppositionalism with evidentialism. Mayers proposes a modified or contemporary Thomism as a solution to what he sees as an apologetical impasse.[1] Norman Geisler, an avowed Protestant Thomist, borrows extensively from Aquinas's metaphysics in order to build his apologetical proofs for God's existence.[2] There

1. Ronald B. Mayers, *Both/And: A Balanced Apologetic* (Chicago: Moody Press, 1984). See esp. chs. 2, 3, and 4 dealing with ontology, epistemology, and theology, respectively. Mayers contends that these three chapters develop his both/and approach, which turns out to be nothing other than a Thomistic apologetic. See my review of this book in the *Westminster Theological Journal* 47, 2 (1985): 354–57.

2. Norman Geisler, *Thomas Aquinas: An Evangelical Appraisal* (Eugene, OR: Wipf & Stock, 2003). See also his *Christian Apologetics* (Grand Rapids: Baker Book House,

have also been those within the Reformed tradition who formulate their theistic proofs within a Thomistic context.[3]

Aquinas's approach to proving God's existence is relevant in contemporary philosophy as well. Contemporary anthologies on the philosophy of religion almost always deal with some version of Thomas's proofs.[4]

Before attempting to summarize the proofs themselves, some preliminary information might be helpful. Aquinas's theistic proofs have come down to us as the *"quinque viae"* or the "five ways." Although Thomas himself speaks of them in this way, he, as well as his followers, never meant to suggest that these five ways had a set number or order. Aquinas presented his proofs succinctly and most simply in his *Summa theologica*, but he never again wrote of them as "five ways," nor did he present them in the same order as in the *ST*. The *ST* was meant to be an introductory study, and therefore it does not present the proofs as thoroughly as might be expected in another context.[5] In the *ST*, he seeks to present each of the five proofs in a short and concise paragraph.

In the *Summa contra gentiles*, however, because it seems to have been written, in part at least, as a manual of apologetics for missionaries,[6] the proofs are presented in more detail than in the *ST*. In the *Summa contra gentiles*, Aquinas divides the "first way," which he considers to be the most important, into two

---

1976), esp. 237–59.

3. R. C. Sproul, John H. Gerstner, and Arthur Lindsley, *Classical Apologetics* (Grand Rapids: Zondervan, 1984), esp. 24–92, 109–36.

4. See, for example, Michael L. Peterson, *Philosophy of Religion: Selected Readings* (New York: Oxford University Press, 1996).

5. See Étienne Gilson, *The Philosophy of St. Thomas Aquinas*, ed. G. A. Erlington (New York: Dorset, 1971), 66.

6. Thomas Aquinas, *Summa Contra Gentiles*, trans. Anton C. Pegis (book 1) et al., 4 vols. in 5 (Notre Dame, IN: University of Notre Dame Press, 1975), introduction to book 1.

arguments, deletes the "third way" of the *ST*, but includes the other three.[7]

In *De potentia*, Aquinas presents the proofs under three heads: one from Plato, one from Aristotle, and one from Avicenna.[8] In his *Compendium theologiae*, Aquinas offers one proof from the argument from motion.[9]

Thus, while Thomists disagree as to whether Thomas's proofs are all reducible to one, there is no disagreement about the fact that such proofs were never, in Thomas's own mind, fixed for the Christian apologist. Thomas used his proofs as the occasion dictated.[10]

Because Thomas's proofs are so flexible, both in presentation and in number, it would seem that there should be some unifying principle lying behind them that would help us see their coherence and perhaps even their validity. We will look more closely at that below.

Since Aquinas set forth his proofs in different ways at different times, we will consider them here as given to us in his *ST*.[11]

7. Ibid., 1:85–86. See also Joseph Owens, *An Elementary Christian Metaphysics* (Milwaukee: Bruce, 1963), 342n30.

8. Aquinas, *Summa Contra Gentiles*, 1:85–86.

9. Ibid.

10. See Étienne Gilson, *Elements of Christian Philosophy* (New York: Doubleday, 1959), 56. Gilson cites one example of Aquinas's own flexibility with the proofs: "What serves as proof of the existence of God in one of Aquinas's works can very well become a proof of one of His attributes in another one. To quote only one striking instance, the admirable Disputed Question *De Potentia*, q.3, a.5, establishes that there can be nothing that is not created by God. Obviously, to prove such a conclusion is tantamount to proving that there is a God. Moreover, the three reasons alleged by Thomas Aquinas in favor of this conclusion rest upon the deepest among his own metaphysical doctrines. Still, what he is proving in this text is not that there is a God, but rather that the true notion of God as prime cause excuses the possibility that anything can exist without being created by Him."

11. The best concise summary of Thomas's proofs can be found in Matthew Levering, *Proofs of God: Classical Arguments from Tertullian to Barth* (Grand Rapids: Baker Academic, 2016), 57–69. The reason, it seems, that Aquinas's "five ways" are widely discussed is that in other works, though the proofs are not set forth in the

The "first way" of Aquinas, called by him "the clearest proof," is the argument from motion or change:[12]

> It is certain, and evident to our senses, that in the world some things are in motion. Now whatever is in motion is put in motion by another, for nothing can be in motion except it is in potentiality to that towards which it is in motion; whereas a thing moves inasmuch as it is in act. For motion is nothing else than the reduction of something from potentiality to actuality. But nothing can be reduced from potentiality to actuality, except by something in a state of actuality.[13]

Aquinas is here borrowing heavily from Aristotle.[14] He takes the potentiality-actuality schema of Aristotle from the physical realm and applies it to the metaphysical realm, the realm of being. Aristotle's primary concern in his argument from motion is not the *existence* of that which is moved or moving, but the *change* that takes place accordingly. Thus, the argument borrowed by Aquinas from Aristotle is in the latter's *Physics*, not his *Metaphysics*. Aquinas, however, seems to be arguing from the perspective of being itself, and only in doing so is he able to conclude with the assertion that there is an Unmoved Mover.

Thus, for Aquinas, the potency-act schema is translated into a metaphysical context and utilized as a proof for God's existence. Aristotle, on the other hand, took existence for granted and thus his four classes of cause (formal, material, efficient, and

---

same way, they are not changed substantially. A summary of the five ways, then, will apply to any other proof or set of proofs that Aquinas employed.

12. Aquinas never used the word "change" for this argument, but it is summarized in that way, for example, in Owens, *An Elementary Christian Metaphysics*, 343.

13. Aquinas, *ST*, I q.2 a.3 resp.

14. See, e.g., Aristotle, *Physics*, bk. 7, ch. 1, 242a, in Aristotle, *The Basic Works of Aristotle*, ed. Richard McKeon (New York: Random House, 1968), 340.

final) are limited to that which brings about change in an already existing being.[15]

Although Aquinas insisted that we must indeed begin with that which appeals to our senses (i.e., the physical), he was just as insistent that the physical leads us, on the basis of "pure philosophy" and "natural reason," to the metaphysical. Such an approach was never delineated by Aristotle in that particular way. When Aquinas speaks, therefore, of the potency-limiting-act principle in his proofs, we are to read this principle primarily as metaphysical, not as referring to the physical.

Notice Aquinas's first premise in this first proof. He begins, as he always does, with sense experience—he has no room for the *a priori* in his proofs. From the observation of data, Aquinas moves to observed change or motion in that data. He is speaking here of "accidental" change—that is, changes that take place, not in the substance of that which we see, but in all of those qualities that are changeable, such as shape, color, and taste. These changes are apparent to sense experience.

The second premise of this "first way" is not apparent to sense experience and thus must be shown.[16] It asserts that whatever is moved is moved by another. In other words, employing the potency-act schema, Aquinas seeks to demonstrate that whatever is changed or moved is not in itself the agent of change, but is changed or moved by that which actually possesses the accidental quality communicated to the patient. "It is therefore impossible," says Thomas, "that in the same respect and in the same way a thing should be both mover and moved, i.e., that it should move itself."[17] He uses the example of fire which (being hot in act) makes the wood (which is hot in potency) actually hot. Wood does not have

---

15. Charles A. Hart, *Thomistic Metaphysics: An Inquiry into the Act of Existing* (Englewood Cliffs, NJ: Prentice-Hall, 1959), 246.

16. Owens, *An Elementary Christian Metaphysics*, 344.

17. Aquinas, *ST*, I q.2 a.3 resp.

the ability to make itself hot. Changes that are communicated to different things must, therefore, be extrinsic to those things.

Aquinas then proceeds to deny an infinite series of movements:

> If that by which it is put in motion be itself put in motion, then this also must needs be put in motion by another, and that by another again. But this cannot go on to infinity, because then there would be no first mover, and, consequently, no other mover.[18]

Gilson sees Aristotle's direct influence on Aquinas here.[19] Aquinas, in this proof, must have been convinced by Aristotle's arguments and therefore saw no need to elaborate on them. Thus, Aquinas deems it apparent that God is this Unmoved Mover.

Owens, following Gilson's new interpretation of Thomas, sees Aquinas's "first way" as a *theological* (rather than *philosophical*) argument:

> If you ask why the immobile movent to which it concludes is recognized at once as God, the answer is to be found in the *Sed Contra* of the article. There God is described in the words of *Exodus* as *I am who I am*, understood as meaning that his very nature is to exist. To all who know the God of Scripture, then, his identity with the immobile movent reached by the argument from motion is at once apparent.[20]

We will remember, from our discussion above, that the new interpretation of Thomas sees this text from Exodus as the beginning point of Thomas's discussion of being.

18. Ibid.
19. Gilson, *The Philosophy of St. Thomas Aquinas*, 70.
20. Owens, *An Elementary Christian Metaphysics*, 345.

As McInerny demonstrates, however, this passage in Thomas is in keeping with his "preambles of the faith," and thus is meant to be understood philosophically, first of all, and not theologically. The quotation from Exodus is in no way meant to impinge on the purely philosophical process in which Aquinas, following Aristotle, engages in this proof. It is not sufficient simply to quote a Bible verse; Thomas should have argued and shown how the content of revelation grounded his arguments. Instead, he bases them on natural reason, which, as we have seen him argue, all people have in the same way.

The "second way" of Aquinas is the way of efficient causality:

> In the world of sense we find there is an order of efficient causes. There is no case known (neither is it, indeed, possible) in which a thing is found to be the efficient cause of itself; for so it would be prior to itself, which is impossible.[21]

Aquinas again seems to borrow from Aristotle in this proof, though Aristotle (*contra* Avicenna and Albertus Magnus) never used this proof as an argument for God's existence.[22] While the first way deals with the being of things that have changed, the second way deals with the cause of substantial being through secondary means.

Those familiar with the radical empiricism of David Hume would, of course, look askance at Aquinas's causal argument. It does seem clear, however, that Aquinas saw cause and effect as empirically observable in the same way that he contends for the observation, or at least the extrapolation from observation, of being or existence.[23]

---

21. Aquinas, *ST*, I q.2 a.3 resp.

22. Gilson, *The Philosophy of St. Thomas Aquinas*, 81.

23. For further elucidation of the principle of cause and effect in the second proof, see Gilson, *Elements of Christian Philosophy*, 69.

Aquinas is concerned to show that the being of a particular thing is caused by that which has being in itself. Because he is discussing substantial, not accidental, being, the second way is not as obvious to sense experience, according to Aquinas, as is the first.

Aquinas continues his proof by arguing again against the notion of an infinite regress. Therefore, it is necessary to admit a first efficient cause, to which everyone gives the name of God.[24] Though the second way tends to apply the same principles as the first, Thomists contend that it is a self-sufficient proof and able to stand on its own.[25]

The "third way" of Aquinas argues from necessary and possible existence:

> We find in nature things that are possible to be and not to be, since they are found to be generated, and to corrupt, and consequently, they are possible to be and not to be. But it is impossible for these always to exist, for that which is possible not to be at some time is not. Therefore, if everything is possible not to be, then at one time there could have been nothing in existence. Now if this were true, even now there would be nothing in existence, because that which does not exist only begins to exist by something already existing. Therefore, if at one time nothing was in existence, it would have been impossible for anything to have begun to exist; and thus even now nothing would be in existence—which is absurd.[26]

It is not difficult to see where Aquinas is going with this argument. He begins again with that which is observed, that is, the contingency of existing beings. Possibility and necessity, for

24. Aquinas, *ST*, I q.2 a.3 resp.

25. See Gilson, *Elements of Christian Philosophy*, 71–72, and Owens, *An Elementary Christian Metaphysics*, 346.

26. Aquinas, *ST*, I q.2 a.3 resp.

Aquinas, are, at least in the beginning of this proof, abstract terms used to describe the observable fact that some things come into existence and others die.[27] The argument turns on the contingency of secondary being, which requires something necessary. Aquinas states at the conclusion of the third way:

> Therefore we cannot but postulate the existence of some being having of itself its own necessity, and not receiving it from another, but rather causing in others their necessity. This all men speak of as God.[28]

The point of the argument seems to be that, while we perceive contingency in those things that exist, we also perceive that something necessary is required for the rationale of the contingency that surrounds us. Necessary existence, for Aquinas, seems to be tantamount to "being."[29] That which has its being conferred by another exists, not in and of itself, which is the reason for its contingency, but because of another who conferred such existence. Aquinas puts this in the context of his metaphysical potency-act schema:

> Hence the potency to not-being in spiritual creatures and the heavenly bodies is rather in God, who can withdraw his influence, than in the form or the matter of such creatures.[30]

In keeping with his metaphysical structure, then, Aquinas supposes that for anything to have being, though temporal, there

27. See Gilson, *Elements of Christian Philosophy*, 72.

28. Aquinas, *ST*, I q.2 a.3 resp.

29. Gilson, *Elements of Christian Philosophy*, 14.

30. Aquinas, *ST*, I q.104 a.1 ad 1: "*Unde potentia ad non esse in spiritualibus creaturis, et corporibus coelestibus magis est in Deo, qui potest subtrahere suum influxum, quam in forma, vel in materia talium creaturarum*," quoted by Owens, *An Elementary Christian Metaphysics*, 149n10.

must be one in whom being is intrinsic. It is, therefore, an argument from temporal to eternal existence, rather than from bare possibility to necessity in being.

The "fourth way" of Aquinas has been described by some as the only truly metaphysical argument.[31] Aquinas argues from degrees found in things to degrees of being, concluding with the ultimate cause of being, which we call God. Things are said to be more and less because they approximate in different degrees to that which is greatest:

> The fourth way is taken from the gradation to be found in things. Among beings there are some more and some less good, true, noble, and the like. But "more" and "less" are predicated of different things, according as they resemble in their different ways something which is the maximum. . . . Now the maximum in any genus is the cause of all in that genus; as fire, which is the maximum of heat, is the cause of all hot things. Therefore there must also be something which is to all beings the cause of their being, goodness, and every other perfection; and this we call God.[32]

This argument appears to be taken both from Aristotle and from Plato.[33] It has been subjected to much scrutiny and to various interpretations. Some have had concerns that Aquinas has bowed the knee to *a priorism* in this proof and has significantly strayed from the moderate realism that seems to characterize his other proofs.[34]

31. See, for example, Gilson, *The Philosophy of St. Thomas Aquinas*, 86–92.
32. Aquinas, *ST*, I q.2 a.3 resp.
33. See Owens, *An Elementary Christian Metaphysics*, 348n44; Gilson, *Elements of Christian Philosophy*, 76; Gilson, *The Philosophy of St. Thomas Aquinas*, 91.
34. Gilson, in the citations above, discusses what he deems to be some predominant misinterpretations of Aquinas's fourth way and posits his own analysis. In my own study of the Thomistic proofs, I was convinced at one point that this fourth

It seems more appropriate, however, to interpret Aquinas here in the light of the other four proofs unless there is obvious reason to do otherwise. Thus, we see Aquinas, in this proof, reasoning from the relative to the absolute, beginning *a posteriori*, that is, with those sensible things that possess certain characteristics in a relative way. Given the existence of those attributes, there must be an absolute that alone would be able to confer such characteristics.

Because Aquinas is constructing a metaphysical argument, as is clear from his citation of Aristotle's *Metaphysics* in this proof, he proceeds from the visible to the notion of being. This argument may more strongly point to Aquinas's principle of participation, individuation, existential metaphysic, and the like, but it does carry through the same basic principles of the other proofs, especially that the created world points to its Creator. We suggest, then, that the proof itself is in accordance with the principles of the others, though perhaps more implicitly metaphysical in character.

The "fifth way" of Aquinas is the argument from providence, or, as he puts it, from "the governance of things":

> The fifth way is taken from the governance of the world. We see that things which lack intelligence, such as natural bodies, act for an end, and this is evident from their acting always, or nearly always, in the same way, so as to obtain the best result. Hence it is plain that not fortuitously, but designedly, do they achieve their end. Now whatever lacks intelligence cannot move towards an end, unless it be directed by some being endowed with knowledge and intelligence; as the arrow

---

way was indeed foundational to, and preeminent among, the others. Since that time, however, I have come to believe that there is something deeper going on in the proofs themselves that may be clearer in the fourth way, but is nevertheless behind the entirety of Thomas's apologetic. We hope to make that clear below.

is shot to its mark by the archer. Therefore some intelligent being exists by whom all natural things are directed to their end; and this being we call God.[35]

This proof is often subsumed under the rubric of the "teleo-logical" argument, and in some sense it is. Yet Owens correctly argues that it is primarily metaphysical, not teleological.[36] Aquinas is arguing in this proof, not merely that there is design, but that the things of this natural realm are being moved to a meaningful end by an Intelligence. It is, in effect, at least to some extent, an addendum to the second way.

Aquinas is concerned to prove, not a Designer, but an Ultimate Efficient Cause, who is intelligently moving those things that are without intelligence toward a meaningful end. Thus, Aquinas is operating in a far different realm than, for example, William Paley, whose teleological argument became the standard.[37] Again, it is metaphysics that provides the foundation for Aquinas's proofs, not simply observation or experience.

With that in mind, we need to look briefly at the metaphysical system that informs Thomas's proofs, as we transition to the next section on "Who God Is." As with everything we have said thus far, we cannot do full justice to the complexity and depth of Thomas's metaphysical system here. We can, however, provide a useful focus of that system in order better to evaluate its weaknesses.

In his discussion of archetypal and ectypal knowledge in Reformed thought, Richard Muller notes,

The basic question to be answered . . . concerns the nature of the relationship between the divine archetype and the temporal ectype: is the relationship such that we can *ascend by*

35. Aquinas, *ST*, I q.2 a.3 resp.
36. Owens, *An Elementary Christian Metaphysics*, 349n46.
37. Ibid.

analogy from what is known here to a clear vision of God—the *analogia entis*—or is the relationship such that we cannot conceive for ourselves a perfect theology?[38]

In this, Muller highlights the metaphysical *analogia entis* (analogy of being), which is one of the key aspects of Thomas's proofs. In order to understand Thomas on analogy, it is necessary to note the central tenets of his notion of "being."

For Aquinas, being is *act* in distinction from essence that is potential existence or *potency*. Being, by definition, is pure actuality. Thus, Aquinas sees existence as at the root of the real.[39] It is the one attribute or characteristic that is common to all things and thus is, in Aquinas's system, a transcendental notion. That is, it transcends the limitations and imperfections of every particular thing that exists.

Aquinas's metaphysics, then, begins with the primacy of existence over essence. It is existence which confers on an essence its "being" or "act of existing." Aquinas seeks to delineate this, very simply, by asserting that we can know what a thing is without asserting its actual existence.[40] Because we can conceptualize, for example, a unicorn, without asserting its actual existence, there must be a distinction between a thing's essence, in this case a unicorn, and its existence. This, it seems, is Aquinas's most basic metaphysical presupposition, which underlies each of his five ways.

Given Aquinas's distinction between existence and essence, he seeks to show that every thing participates in its "received act of to be" (i.e., "being") only to the degree that its respective

---

38. Richard A. Muller, *Post-Reformation Reformed Dogmatics: The Rise and Development of Reformed Orthodoxy, ca. 1520 to ca. 1725*, vol. 1, *Prolegomena to Theology*, 2nd ed. (Grand Rapids: Baker Academic, 2003), 227.

39. Gilson, *The Philosophy of St. Thomas Aquinas*, 34.

40. See, e.g., Aquinas, "On Being and Essence," in *Selected Writings of St. Thomas Aquinas*, trans. Robert P. Goodwin (Indianapolis: Bobbs-Merrill, 1965), 54.

essence permits. This is the Aristotelian potency-limiting-act principle in natural philosophy, translated by Aquinas into the science of metaphysics. In Thomas's metaphysics, potentiality limits actuality. That is, essence is potential existence. Essence is not in itself existence and therefore does not have existence in itself. When the perfection of being, which is inherently unlimited and transcendental, confers existence on an essence, that which is unlimited and transcendental becomes limited and actual only to the degree that a thing's essence will permit.

It must be remembered in this discussion that Aquinas always maintained that our knowledge comes to us by way of sensory experience. As we experience reality through our senses, we recognize that certain things both exist and are diverse, which enables us to postulate this metaphysical theory. Being, as inherently unlimited and as the "act of to be," is limited and actualized through essences.

This combination, according to Aquinas, can be neither a synthetic nor a part/whole relationship. Such is the case because both synthetic and part/whole relationships require that there be three things: the act of existing, the essence of that which exists, and the thing itself. A combination of this sort would require something above and beyond each part, as well as the whole, that is more actual, more perfect.

Yet Aquinas has already asserted that being is the most perfect of all perfections and is in itself actuality. There can be nothing that is more existent than being or more perfect than being. Any synthetic or part/whole relationship would require as much. For Aquinas, the relationship between being and essence could be called a transcendental relation due to the fact that it must transcend every lesser relationship.[41]

41. Hart, *Thomistic Metaphysics*, 88. For an example of the synthetic relationship, e.g., in the composition of body and soul, see Aquinas, *Summa contra gentiles*, vol. 3, ch. 80.

This metaphysical construct gives us the backdrop for Aquinas's view of analogy, which, again, relates directly to his theistic proofs. It is difficult to find a consensus among Thomistic scholars as to Aquinas's own teaching on analogy. Such is the case, in part, because this crucial doctrine was never set out by Aquinas in systematic form. There is no "chapter" in Thomas's writings on analogy.

However, there is widespread agreement that Aquinas did teach what has come to be known as the "analogy of proper proportionality."[42] Analogy of proper proportionality is a metaphysical notion designed to articulate the fact that being *itself* cannot be seen, but is "perceived" *in each thing* in proportion to its essence.[43] A thing is said to "be" in proportion to its nature. Thus, the being of a man is in some sense similar to the being of a rock and in some sense dissimilar. There is, then, an analogy of proper proportionality between the rock and the man.

As one can see, this analogy is based on the distinction already noted between existence and essence. Phelan maintains that there are only three ways to conceive of any proportional analogy. The first is that the common character or *ratio* belongs really and truly to each participant in the same way but in unequal

42. Ralph M. McInerny, in *The Logic of Analogy: An Interpretation of St. Thomas* (The Hague: Martinus Nijhoff, 1961), argues for Thomistic analogy as a logical rather than metaphysical construct. If he is right, then proper proportionality relates primarily to terms rather than to things. We cannot enter that debate here. We would only interject that, even if McInerny is correct, meaningful predication for Aquinas still depends on his metaphysics, and thus his doctrine of analogy would have significant metaphysical implications. Suffice it to say at this point that Thomas's metaphysics requires his notion of analogy in a symmetrical way, such that if one is altered, so, to a greater or lesser extent, must the other be altered. For this latter point, see Scott MacDonald, "Theory of Knowledge," in *The Cambridge Companion to Aquinas*, ed. Norman Kretzmann and Eleonore Stump (Cambridge: Cambridge University Press, 1993), 160–95.

43. G. B. Phelan, *Saint Thomas and Analogy* (Milwaukee: Marquette University Press, 1941), 8.

degrees. The second is that the *ratio* belongs really to only one participant but is attributed to others. The third is that the *ratio* belongs really and truly to each participant, but only in proportion to their being.[44] This third analogy, of course, is the analogy of proper proportionality and is the analogy used by Thomas. It must always deal with the relation of existence and essence in a thing and thus is, by definition, proportional.[45]

In the analogy of proper proportionality, Aquinas seeks to distinguish between the same *attributes* in different *things*. He denies univocal predication because of God's coterminous character.[46] That is, because that which is ascribed to creatures or creation is ascribed in a divided and particular way, and because the same ascription would be simple and universal in God (because God is what he thinks and thinks what he is—see the next section), such ascription to both cannot be univocal.

But Aquinas must also deny equivocal predication.[47] There is indeed a certain likeness of creation to its Creator, though such likeness can never be predicated univocally. Equivocation would show us that though one name is predicated of several things, we cannot infer from one of those things the knowledge of the other because there is, by definition, no point of reference. We could, therefore, understand nothing of God from creation, which for Aquinas is patently false.

Thus, as Aquinas develops his doctrine of analogy, he argues that that which is predicated of both God and man actually exists in both to the extent that their respective essences permit. To say that "God is good" and that "man is good" is to say that God is good in proportion to his "received act of to be" (which *only*

44. Ibid.

45. Aquinas's doctrine of analogy is found, among other places, in *ST*, 1, Q. 13, *De veritate*, Q. 2, and, for our purposes here, in *Summa contra gentiles*, book 1, chs. 25–33.

46. See Aquinas, *Summa contra gentiles*, book 1, ch. 32.

47. See ibid., book 1, ch. 33.

in God is his essence) and that man is good with respect to his potential existence. Or, to use another example, God knows as God, and man knows as man. The proportion that obtains between being and essence determines the proper predication of that which characterizes each thing.

We begin to see something here of Aquinas's "scale of being."[48] Every thing is limited in being in accordance with its essence. Every characteristic of a thing is further limited as to the proportion that obtains between its being and its essence. Thus, potential existence limits the received act of to be (existence), and the combination of the two, in a particular thing, limits the attributes and perfections of that which is. We could say then that angels *know* as angels *are*, men *know* as men *are*, and there is a proportion (1) between knowledge in angels as they exist and (2) between knowledge in angels and knowledge in men. Knowledge, therefore, cannot be predicated in the same way when speaking of an angel's knowledge and a man's knowledge, the existences of such being proportional to their respective essences.

But there is a tension within this Thomistic doctrine that has caused some controversy among his interpreters. Simply stated (and on this all seem to agree), *the analogy of proper proportionality cannot really apply to God.* The reason for this is that the analogy of proper proportionality derives its basis from the *proportion* that obtains between essence and existence. But in God no such proportion obtains. God is pure act. His essence *is* his existence. Unlike any other thing, it belongs to the very essence of God to exist. How, then, can a real, proportional analogy be predicated of men, in which every act of existence is limited by essence, and God, in which essence and existence are identical and completely exhaustive of each other? It seems, then, that a second

---

48. See, for example, Cornelius Van Til, *Christianity in Conflict*, 3 vols. (unpublished syllabus, 1962), vol. 2, pt. 2, ch. 3.

kind of analogy must be introduced that will account for the one in whom essence and existence are identical. Such an analogy has been called the "analogy of intrinsic attribution"[49] and can be seen, for example, in the following statement from Aquinas:

> Therefore it must be said that these names are said of God and creatures in an analogous sense, that is, according to proportion. Now names are thus used in two ways: either according as many things are proportionate to one, . . . or according as one thing is proportionate to another, thus *healthy* is said of medicine and animal, since medicine is the cause of health in the animal body. . . . Thus, whatever is said of God and creatures, is said according to *the relation of a creature to God as its principle and cause*, wherein all perfections of things pre-exist excellently. Now this mode of community of idea is a mean between pure equivocation and simple univocation. For in analogies the idea is not, as it is in univocals, one and the same, yet it is not totally diverse as in equivocals; but a term which is thus used in a multiple sense signifies various proportions to some one thing. . . . Therefore the universal cause of the whole species is not an univocal agent: and the universal cause comes before the particular cause. But this universal agent, whilst it is not univocal, nevertheless is not altogether equivocal, otherwise it could not produce its own likeness, but rather it is to be called an analogical agent, as all univocal predications are reduced to one first non-univocal analogical predication, which is *being*.[50]

---

49. The distinction between analogy of proportionality and intrinsic attribution comes from Cajetan. Because, as we have seen, Cajetan's interpretation of Thomas has become highly suspect in the new view of Thomas, so also are these two aspects of Thomas's view of analogy. See, for example, James F. Anderson, *Reflections on the Analogy of Being* (The Hague: Martinus Nijhoff, 1967).

50. Aquinas, *ST*, I q.13 a.5 ad 1 (emphases added).

Note the absence (conceptually, not terminologically) of any proportionality in this statement. Such is the case because Aquinas is now attempting to do justice to analogical predication with respect to the Creator. This analogy of intrinsic attribution, therefore, has as its basis, not the *proportionality* of things, but their *causal* relation. The relation of creature to God in the above quote is a causal relation, yet is described as an analogical relationship. Because the definition of potential existence is that which makes a thing what it is, what is of the essence of a thing must be possessed fully by that thing. For example, it is impossible for man to be partly human. It follows, then, for Aquinas, that existence is not intrinsic to created being and therefore must be caused by the one in whom essence and existence are identical. The analogy of intrinsic attribution becomes, then, in one sense, the basis for Thomas's proofs, as well as for his analogy of proper proportionality.[51] As Hart explains,

> Analogy of intrinsic attribution, then, will assure us that between limited beings of our direct experience, in whom there is a real relation between essence and existence and a conceivable being in whom there is no such real relation, but identity of essence and existence, there is still real similarity. By our analogy of proper proportionality we can then assert of this latter being, as actually intrinsically possessed, in an unlimited way, all those perfections that we found proportionately in finite beings of our actual experience, with an assurance that only an analogy of attribution can provide.[52]

---

51. Such is the case because the creature's relationship to God must be the foundation for his relationship to other beings, the latter of which is the concern of analogy of proper proportionality. Whether or not one agrees with Aquinas's second "analogy," i.e., that of intrinsic attribution, one must still meet the demand of explaining to some extent the creature's relationship to God.

52. Hart, *Thomistic Metaphysics*, 42.

Thus, while analogy of extrinsic attribution is foreign to Aquinas's thinking, because in such the analogon really exists in only one of the analogates of which it is predicated, analogy of intrinsic attribution is affirmed because "being" is caused by, and thus is intrinsic to, all analogates.[53] Both analogies, of proper proportionality and of intrinsic attribution, seem necessary to deal with the relationship of God to his world.

Our knowledge of God, then, is always analogical. It depends on the analogy of being (*analogia entis*), as well as on the causality of God. In this sense, the proofs are all extensions of Thomas's view of analogy. They presuppose the *analogia entis* and are rooted in God's causal activity, as that activity is supposedly demonstrated from the reality of cause and effect in the world. We will see, in the "Critique" below, in the discussion of "Proofs of God's Existence," that this is an insufficient structure for such proofs.

Who God Is

Our discussion here will be limited, but it is possible to get to the heart of Thomas's natural "theology proper." In order to understand the doctrine of God, obtained through natural reason alone, according to Aquinas, the central focus must be on God's simplicity. As a matter of fact, according to Eleonore Stump, the simplicity of God, for Aquinas, "is foundational for everything in Aquinas's thought from his metaphysics to his ethics."[54]

Thomas begins his discussion of God's simplicity in this way:

> When the existence of a thing has been ascertained there remains the further question of the manner of its existence,

53. Ibid., 39.
54. Eleonore Stump, *Aquinas* (London: Routledge, 2003), 92.

in order that we may know its essence. Now, because we cannot know what God is, but rather what He is not, we have
no means for considering how God is, but rather how He is
not. . . . Now it can be shown how God is not, by denying of
Him whatever is opposed to the idea of Him—viz., composition, motion, and the like.[55]

There are eight aspects to God's simplicity that Thomas wants
to evaluate:

> Concerning His simplicity, there are eight points of inquiry:
> (1) Whether God is a body? (2) Whether He is composed
> of matter and form? (3) Whether in Him there is composi-
> tion of quiddity, essence or nature, and subject? (4) Whether
> He is composed of essence and existence? (5) Whether He is
> composed of genus and difference? (6) Whether He is com-
> posed of subject and accident? (7) Whether He is in any way
> composite, or wholly simple? (8) Whether He enters into
> composition with other things?[56]

In the interest of space, we will leave the more obvious aspects
aside. Except for certain cults, few would affirm (1), (2), or (3)
of God; each of them suppose that God is material in some way.
We will briefly summarize (4), (5), (7), and (8). We will then
lay out Thomas's denial of (6), so that, in the "Critique" below,
in the discussion of "Who God Is," we may focus on some of its
insufficiencies.

In (4), Thomas argues that God's existence and essence
are identical. Because, as we noted above, Thomas sees a real
distinction between existence and essence, any essence that

---

55. Aquinas, *ST*, I q.3.
56. Ibid.

exists must have that existence caused by something else. "But this cannot be true of God; because we call God the first efficient cause."[57] In God, therefore, essence and existence must be identical.

In (5), Thomas then affirms that God is not contained in a category of "genus," for three reasons. "First, because a species is constituted of genus and difference."[58] Here Thomas makes it clear that when we use the word "God," we are not referring to one who is a specific instance of something more generic. If that were so, then God would be included in a category with others of the same genus.

Secondly, Thomas argues that if God were to be included in a genus, it would have to be the genus "being." But the Philosopher has shown (*Metaph.* iii) that being cannot be a genus, for every genus has differences distinct from its generic essence. Now no difference can exist distinct from being, for nonbeing cannot be a difference. It follows then that God is not in a genus.[59]

Thirdly, God cannot be in a genus because then there would be both generic identity and essential differences. "For the existence of man and of horse is not the same; as also of this man and that man: thus in every member of a genus, existence and quiddity—i.e., essence—must differ."[60] It cannot be true of God, in other words, that his existence would be generically related to, though essentially different from, other things in a genus. This would deny the absolute uniqueness of God.

Though (7) and (8) contain some nuances of previous arguments, essentially they repeat the reasons why it must be the case that God is simple.

In (6), Thomas rightly argues that God cannot be composed

57. Ibid., I q.3 a.4.
58. Ibid., I q.3 a.5 resp.
59. Ibid.
60. Ibid.

of subject and accident, for the following reasons.[61] First, if God were a subject composed of accidents, then he would not be complete in himself. He would need something else—something not essential to him—in order to be properly identified, "for a subject is in some sense made actual by its accidents. But there can be no potentiality in God." Secondly, if God were composed of subject and accident, he would not be absolute. He would have something added to him in order to make him what he is. This, we can see, is similar to Thomas's first reason. In this second reason, however, we should see that Thomas wants to deny that anything relative is added to God's existence and character. Thirdly, says Thomas, God cannot have any essential accidents because such accidents would somehow have to be caused in God. But, as Thomas has argued, "There can be nothing caused in God, since He is the first cause. Hence it follows that there is no accident in God."[62]

For Thomas, the simplicity of God follows from his absolute character. If God is *a se*, there can be nothing on which he depends in order to be who he is. To be independent and absolute means that God is complete in himself. He is, as Thomas puts it, pure actuality (*actus purus*). He is pure actuality because there can be no potentiality in God. If there were, then he would be in need of something else in order to be God.

This view of the simplicity of God is a central aspect of Thomas's natural theology; it is the focus of natural reason's demonstration of God's character. For Thomas, it is central to everything else he teaches. We will reserve further discussion of it until our "Critique," below, in the section on "Who God Is."

---

61. What follows is my summary of *ST*, I q.3 a.6 resp.
62. See below for Eleonore Stump's assessment of Thomas's view of "accident."

Critique

Proofs of God's Existence

As we begin to assess the "five ways" of Thomas, our concerns will overlap with our critique of Thomas's theology proper, below. As we noted above, the proofs are both epistemological and metaphysical. That is, the proofs are a product of Thomas's view of natural reason, as well as his view of being. So the concerns we express about the proofs will impinge on both.

In order to understand the metaphysical problems embedded in Thomas's proofs, we need first to highlight the epistemological aspects again. We will remember from our discussion in chapter 2 that Thomas insists that natural reason, which is the reasoning capacity of all people, is able to discern God's existence and his simplicity.

Due to Thomas's influence, the paradigm for medieval philosophical theology included a "natural" substructure, that is, "natural reason," upon which a supernatural layer, that is, revelation, could be added. In other words, according to Thomas, there is much truth that can be acquired and demonstrated without any need of revelation, and then there are truths that can only be had by way of special revelation.[63]

But this paradigm was rightly rejected during the time of the Reformation and in seventeenth-century Protestant theology. Because of the importance of Scripture, the Reformers saw *true* natural theology as a product, not of natural reason, but of natural revelation and of a regenerate mind. According to Richard Muller,

> *Theologia naturalis* [natural theology], despite all the problems inherent in its formulation and elaboration, is properly

63. We should note, in this regard, that Richard Muller's assessment of the "five

discussed as a form of *theologia vera* [true theology], under the category of *theologia viatorum* [pilgrim theology]. This placement of the topic arises from the fact that *theologia naturalis* is neither a theology of union nor a theology of vision, but *a theology of revelation*. Since the mode of communication of natural theology is *revelation*, natural theology must be discussed together with supernatural theology. What is more, as indicated by the Reformed orthodox paradigm of true and false, archetypal and ectypal theology, the true, ectypal *theologia naturalis* is founded not on the interaction of reason in general with the natural order (so that it is not to be equated with natural sciences like astronomy or physics) but on the examination of natural revelation by faithful reason.[64]

Natural theology, according to the Reformed, is a product of "pilgrim theology," that is, of the theology of the regenerate. This is the case because the Reformers, following Calvin,

---

ways," which has some affinity with the new view of Thomas discussed in chapter 2, cannot be sustained. According to Muller, "The medieval approaches to the proofs, moreover, virtually never accord with the modern understanding of demonstrations as a matter of apologetics and/or as . . . a prelude or prolegomenon to 'revealed theology' resting on 'natural theology.' Thus, by way of example, Aquinas' 'five ways' belong to theology, specifically, to the faithful exercise of reason rather than to the realm of a purely rational apologetic." Richard A. Muller, *Post-Reformation Reformed Dogmatics: The Rise and Development of Reformed Orthodoxy, ca. 1520 to ca. 1725*, vol. 3, *The Divine Essence and Attributes* (Grand Rapids: Baker Academic, 2003), 48. But Thomas does not attribute his apologetic to Scripture (though he does quote Exodus 3:14, as we have seen). Nor is it a modern view that regards Thomas's five ways as a "prelude to revealed theology." Instead, as we have seen, the notion of philosophical—i.e., "pure nature"—*preambles of the faith* is the historic view, in Thomism and in the Roman church. As we have seen, Thomas argues that all people can reach the truth of God's existence, simplicity, etc. by exercising natural reason alone, because Aristotle has shown that to be the case. This takes the five ways out of the realm of theology and, as McInerny shows, locates them in the preambles to the faith. See also Herman Bavinck, *Reformed Dogmatics*, vol. 1, *Prolegomena*, ed. John Bolt, trans. John Vriend (Grand Rapids: Baker Academic, 2003), 108.

64. Muller, *Post-Reformation Reformed Dogmatics*, 1:282 (emphases added).

understood that reality is exhaustively *revelational*. There is no such thing as the "purely natural." Since the heavens declare the glory of God (Ps. 19:1), since God speaks through all that he has made (Rom. 1:19–20), that which is "natural" is, at the same time, the very "supernatural" communication of God to his creatures. If that communication occurred only through his special revelation, then there would be a need for a natural substructure. But since *all of reality* is revelational, there can be no substructure that is not, at the same time, revealing God and his character to us.

Thomas, however, sees natural reason as that which is given by God to all people, and which can be exercised in the same ways by all. As Thomas develops his proofs, then, the question is this: what categories does natural reason have available to it in order to conclude that God exists?

For example, let us consider the "second way," which concludes that there is a First Cause. What *kind* of First Cause would this be, according to natural reason? Would it be eternal or would it be in some way subject to temporal sequence? Would it be something necessarily correlative to its "effects," or independent of those effects? What principle or principles can natural reason employ in order to answer these questions? In arguing for the necessity of a First Cause, Thomas says,

> Now in efficient causes it is not possible to go on to infinity, because in all efficient causes following in order, the first is the cause of the intermediate cause, and the intermediate is the cause of the ultimate cause, whether the intermediate cause be several, or one only. Now to take away the cause is to take away the effect. Therefore, if there be no first cause among efficient causes, there will be no ultimate, nor any intermediate cause. But if in efficient causes it is possible to go on to infinity, there will be no first efficient cause, neither

will there be an ultimate effect, nor any intermediate efficient causes; all of which is plainly false.[65]

In his assessment of the first, second, and third ways of Aquinas—all of which can be grouped as "cosmological arguments"—Stephen Davis makes a distinction between linear causality and hierarchical causality. He argues that Thomas might have been employing the latter, not the former.[66] A linear cause is one in which the effect is dependent on the cause for its initial existence, but not for its continuation. Thomas clearly would not have had this in mind, since all effects are dependent on God. In hierarchical causality, the cause must exist "at some finite amount of time prior to the existence of its effects."[67] Not only so, but the existence of the effect(s) is, at every point in time, dependent on the cause.

If we import into Thomas's cosmological arguments the notion of hierarchical causality, according to Davis, the argument can be demonstrated as valid.[68] The problem, as Davis recognizes, is that Thomas would not have approved of a First Cause (or a Necessary Being) that exists at some finite amount of time prior to the existence of its effects. Thomas believed in the eternity of God, which means, at least, that God is not subject to a temporal sequence of moments. Yet in order for any version of the cosmological argument to work, the conclusion must presuppose some aspect of temporal causality. That is, the First Cause (or Necessary Being) must be *prior to* its effects.

65. Thomas Aquinas, *ST*, I q.2 a.3 resp.

66. Stephen T. Davis, *God, Reason and Theistic Proofs* (Grand Rapids: Eerdmans, 1997), 60–78. Davis applies this distinction specifically to Thomas's third way, which argues from contingency to necessity, but it applies as well to the second way, in that Thomas refers to the second way in his assertion, in the third way, that an infinite series of causes is impossible.

67. Ibid., 70.

68. Davis lays out his argument, in 27 propositions, ibid., 70–73.

The problem that Thomas's arguments face is that natural reason has available to it only two ways of justifying its principles. There must be either a *logical* principle that requires a First Cause or an *empirical* principle, an experience, that requires it. But what logical principle requires that which is above and beyond time? In what way can logic apply to the eternal (especial when "the eternal" is meant to be God)? Additionally, it cannot be the case that one could have an *experience* of a First Cause. It looks as though natural reason is unable to provide a conclusion that would agree with Thomas's conclusion, "This all men speak of as God."

It might be helpful at this point to witness a modern-day example of Thomistic argumentation. This example will show how someone who does not affirm the existence of God—in this case, a self-avowed humanist—responds to a "First Cause" kind of argument. The response of the humanist helps us to see the internal weakness of the argument. Because the dialog below is taken from an actual transcript, the statements will have a conversational tone. We will denominate the discussion as one between a Christian (C) and a humanist (H).[69] We have edited the discussion in order to focus on the salient points of our analysis of the proofs. The conversation begins:[70]

(H): So, humanism, I think, is the best expression of modern science. It's the scientific outlook, using the rigorous methods of scientific inquiry in order to test hypotheses about nature.

(C): Well, I agree . . . that we need to be rational; we need to be scientific. . . . Now one of the fundamental, rational laws of

69. Both interlocutors would affirm these ascriptions. The Christian in this dialogue is a committed Thomist.

70. This dialogue is an edited version of "Secular Humanism," *The John Ankerberg Show,* Complete Program Transcripts (Chattanooga, TN: John Ankerberg Evangelistic Ministries, 1986), 3–7. The names of the two interlocutors are not

all thought . . . is that every event, everything that comes to be, has a cause.

(H): Well, you said that every event has a cause. You maintain that every event has a cause. Is that what you said?

(C): That's exactly right. Everything that comes to be has a cause.

(H): Okay. Then you say, "The universe has a cause," and I take it that you would say that God caused the universe. My question then is, "If every event has a cause, what caused God?"

(C): You see, you just confused the statement. "Everything that comes to be has a cause." God didn't come to be, so he doesn't need a cause. Just as the atheist believes . . .

(H): You contradicted your notion that everything has a cause.

(C): No I didn't. Let me finish. Just as the atheist believes that the universe is eternal . . . and therefore didn't need a cause, if you can have an uncaused universe, we can have an uncaused God. What's sauce for the goose is sauce for the gander.

Later on, this was said in the conversation:

(H): You're only pushing your ignorance one step back.

(C): No, no, you're missing the point. You're not listening to it.

---

important here, and will remain anonymous, in order to highlight the method itself.

(H): I'm listening to everything.

(C): Everything that comes to be has a cause . . . that's the principle. The universe came to be, therefore the universe has a cause. Now, if God always existed, he didn't "come to be."

(H): He did not come to be. I see.

(C): He doesn't need a cause.

(H): Well, you're defining the situation. You're assuming your case by definition.

(C): Not at all. The rational person.

(H): How did you know that God did not come to be? How do you know that?

(C): We know that the universe came to be.

(H): But how do you know that God did not come to be?

(C): And we know that everything that comes to be had a cause.

(H): But how did you know that God did not come to be?

(C): Because everything that comes to be has a cause, and if God caused the universe to come to be, he couldn't have come to be.

(H): By definition you're defining . . . you're trying to define what you want to prove. How do you know?

Later on in the conversation:

(H): And now you're leaping beyond the range of observation. You're only pushing your ignorance back one step.

Then, finally:

(C): Well, why is it rational for you to believe that the universe is uncaused, and irrational for me to believe that God is uncaused?

There are a number of things one could say about this dialog, but we will be content here to point out two of the most serious problems. First, notice again how the dialog begins:

(H): So, humanism, I think, is the best expression of modern science. It's the scientific outlook, using the rigorous methods of the scientific inquiry in order to test hypotheses about nature.

(C): Well, I agree . . . that we need to be rational; we need to be scientific. . . . Now one of the fundamental, rational laws of all thought . . . is that every event, everything that comes to be, has a cause.

The humanist sets the stage by affirming his allegiance to "scientific inquiry," by which he means, in part, empirical investigation by way of the natural reason of both interlocutors.

The Christian then attempts to stand on the humanist's ground. He sets his own argument within the context of a supposedly neutral rationality—natural reason—including supposedly neutral "fundamental, rational laws of all thought." In true Thomistic fashion, the Christian has just conceded that his discussion can proceed apace on exactly the same ground that the humanist affirms.

We are not saying that scientific inquiry is useless and always in error. However, when it comes to questions of truth, of the origin of the universe, of evidences for that origin, the scientific inquiry of the humanist will suppress what is obvious and will not see the very facts of inquiry as *God's facts*, in the first place. To concede the starting point to the humanist is to concede the argument altogether (a concession that is obvious in the argument's conclusion).

This leads to our second concern. Notice again what happens toward the end of the discussion. As the Christian moves to the fact of God's uncaused existence, the conversation takes this turn:

(H): How did you know that God did not come to be? How do you know that?

(C): We know that the universe came to be.

(H): But how do you know that God did not come to be?

(C): And we know that everything that comes to be had a cause.

(H): But how did you know that God did not come to be?

(C): Because everything that comes to be has a cause, and if God caused the universe to come to be, he couldn't have come to be.

(H): By definition you're defining . . . you're trying to define what you want to prove. How do you know?

Five times in this short snippet of the dialogue, the humanist asks the epistemological question. He wants to know how it is that the Christian knows that God did not come to be. Notice how the Christian answers the repeated "How do you know?" question. His responses are: "We know that the universe came to be," "And we know that everything that comes to be had a cause," and "Because everything that comes to be has a cause, and if God caused the universe to come to be, he couldn't have come to be." The response of the Christian, in other words, is simply to repeat the argument, over and over again.

But the question being asked by the humanist is a good question, and it goes beyond a mere repetition of the same propositions. It is not a question about the statements already contained in the argument itself. The humanist's question, "How do you know?" relates to the *ground* of the Christian's knowledge about God.

But because the Christian began his discussion by conceding the humanist's starting point, that is, by arguing according to natural reason and therefore supposing that scientific inquiry is based on the same presuppositions for both of them, there is no way for him, now, to move the discussion to another *principium*. In other words, if the Christian has agreed that natural reason is the *principium* for them both, it is not possible for him to jump to biblical revelation as his *principium* when the question of God's character comes into view.

Not only so, but when the Christian says, "If God caused the universe to come to be, he couldn't have come to be," he is assuming, illegitimately, given his admitted ground of scientific inquiry, that the only options available to him and the humanist are either the existence of God as uncaused or the universe as uncaused. But why, we could ask, given scientific inquiry, are these the only two options available? What scientific principle requires that these be the only options?[71] We can sense the struggle of the Christian in this discussion, wanting to affirm Christian principles, but having no access to the only means by which such can be affirmed— that is, God's revelation.

Natural reason, in the way Thomas uses it, does not allow for one who is truly infinite, eternal, and immutable; it certainly does not allow for one who is triune. But with only the triune God that Thomas thinks is demonstrated, the cause and reason for anything that exists remains inexplicable. Thus, there must be some other starting point for these kinds of arguments that can recognize the reality of the Christian God. That starting point can only be the fullness of God's revelation.[72]

Cornelius Van Til laid out for us the root of the problem with these proofs:

> It is in some such fashion that Rome thinks of the natu-ral man. Following Aristotle's general method of reasoning Thomas Aquinas argues that the natural man can, by the ordinary use of his reason, do justice to the natural revelation that surrounds him. He merely needs some assistance in order that he may also see and react properly to the supernat-ural revelation that is found in Christianity.[73]

---

71. Note, for example, Graham Oppy's assessment of final causality: "If we sup-pose that there is a first cause, then there are two options: either it is contingent or it is necessary. If we are theists, the first cause is God; if we are naturalists, the first cause is the initial state of natural reality. . . . Some naturalists suppose that the initial state of natural reality is necessary; other naturalists suppose that it is contingent. If pushed to choose, I would say—albeit with no great confidence—that if there is an initial state of natural reality, then it is necessary." See K. Scott Oliphint, "Covenant Model," in *Four Views on Christianity and Philosophy*, ed. Paul M. Gould and Richard Brian Davis (Grand Rapids: Zondervan, 2016), 101.

72. For an example of how a *revelational* cosmological argument might proceed, see K. Scott Oliphint, *Covenantal Apologetics: Principles and Practice in Defense of Our Faith* (Wheaton, IL: Crossway, 2013), 107–16.

73. Cornelius Van Til, *Defense of the Faith*, 4th ed., ed. K. Scott Oliphint

The outcome of this Thomistic assumption, however, is devastating:

> If Christian revelation, which presupposes the darkness and error of unspiritual humanity, *submitted in advance to the judgments of reason*, it would by that token contradict itself. *It would thereby place itself before a tribunal whose jurisdiction it had first denied.* And having once recognized the authority of reason on the level of *first principles* [*principia*], it could no longer oppose that authority in the articles of faith. Dualistic supernaturalism always has to lead to rationalism, inasmuch it is rationalistic in principle.[74]

As Thomas himself said, "A small error at the beginning of something is a great one at the end."[75] For Thomas, the "small error" was to assume that Aristotle and the philosophers who were able to reason their way to theism had proceeded in the proper way. The "great error" that showed itself in the end was that only a finite and temporal god could be its conclusion.

Who God Is

In this section, we will confine ourselves to a discussion of Thomas's view of God's simplicity and its implications. Before we focus specifically on Thomas, however, it is necessary to recognize that the simplicity of God rightly became a confessional doctrine for Protestants. The *Westminster Confession of Faith*, for example, in chapter 2, affirms that God is "without body, parts, or passions." This is the Confession's way of describing

---

(Phillipsburg, NJ: P&R Publishing, 2008), 110.

74. Bavinck, *Reformed Dogmatics*, 1:516 (emphasis added).

75. Thomas Aquinas, "On Being and Essence," in *Selected Writings of St. Thomas Aquinas*, trans. Robert P. Goodwin (Indianapolis: Bobbs-Merrill, 1965), 33. The original: "*Quia parvus error in principio magnus est in fine.*"

the simplicity of God. With respect to who he is as God, he can have no parts, he can have no body, and he can have no passions. Christianity has always recognized this as an important truth. According to Richard Muller, citing numerous sources, "The doctrine of divine simplicity is among the normative assumptions of theology from the time of the church fathers, to the age of the great medieval scholastic systems, to the era of Reformation and post-Reformation theology, and indeed, on into the succeeding era of late orthodoxy and rationalism."[76] Because the doctrine of divine simplicity is so central in Thomas's natural theology, however, it is important to analyze it from that perspective.

The first thing that must be said is that natural reason alone provides no reason to believe in divine simplicity. There certainly is no empirical basis that can support it, and there can be no rational reason to affirm it, unless one presupposes the triune God at the outset. The best one can hope for with a natural theology of simplicity is that the concept *could* apply to a god, if one existed.[77] But no rationale can be given for the ascription of simplicity to a god of natural theology. There are no categories in "pure nature" that can give rise to such an idea.

But the problems of simplicity do not dissolve if one denies the existence of natural reason and the philosophical preambles of pure nature that are purported, by Thomas, to demonstrate it. Even when we assume the existence of the triune God of Christianity, the notion of simplicity remains enigmatic.

---

76. Richard A. Muller, *Post-Reformation Reformed Dogmatics*, 3:39. We should also note that, at least according to Gavin Ortlund, there is no *consensus fidelium* with respect to divine simplicity. See Gavin Ortlund, "Divine Simplicity in Historical Perspective: Resourcing a Contemporary Discussion," *International Journal of Systematic Theology* 16, 4 (2014): 436–53.

77. It was the view of Cardinal Cajetan that Thomas's proofs only demonstrated properties that could apply to a god, but not to God himself. See, for example, Igor Agostini, "Descartes's Proofs of God and the Crisis of Thomas Aquinas's Five Ways

Perhaps one of the most significant challenges to the doctrine of divine simplicity has come from Alvin Plantinga. In 1980, Plantinga gave the Thomas Aquinas lecture at Marquette University, which was entitled "Does God Have a Nature?"[78] This, of course, is a provocative question. Plantinga notes that, historically, the answer has been yes. However, an affirmative answer could very well deny the doctrine of divine simplicity. Divine simplicity affirms not that God *has* a nature, but that God *is* his nature.

Plantinga wants to answer yes to his question and to argue that God's nature cannot be identical with who he is. Because Plantinga's lecture provides a serious and rigorous challenge to this doctrine, we should at least be aware of its general contents and of possible responses to it.

Plantinga first notes that the doctrine of divine simplicity is "a dark saying indeed."[79] To his credit, he thinks it is a dark saying because if one believes it, one is forced to affirm all kinds of notions that imply the rejection of the Christian God—that God is personal, for example. So, his reason for seeing simplicity as "dark" is the threat he sees it posing to (aspects of) traditional Christianity.

Plantinga's first argument against divine simplicity can be stated fairly simply. If God is identical with his properties—his goodness, wisdom, and holiness, for example—then each of the properties is identical with the other. And if all of the properties are identical, then there is only one property. And if God is identical with that property, then God is a property. This is

---

in Early Modern Thomism: Scholastic and Cartesian Debates," *Harvard Theological Review* 108, 2 (2015): 236.

78. For a detailed analysis and critique of Plantinga's view of simplicity, see F. G. Immink, *Divine Simplicity* (Kampen: Kok, 1987).

79. Alvin Plantinga, "Does God Have a Nature?," in *The Analytic Theist: An Alvin Plantinga Reader*, ed. James F. Sennett (Grand Rapids: Eerdmans, 1998), 228.

Plantinga's first problem, since he does not want to affirm that God is a property; he wants to affirm God as a person, or a personality. Therefore, simplicity has to be rejected.

Plantinga's second problem is a complex web of arguments centering on what he calls the "sovereignty-aseity intuition (SAI)."[80] The SAI basically affirms that God is sovereign over all things and is dependent on nothing at all. Plantinga rightly sees that God's aseity entails his simplicity, but he wants to reject both God's sovereignty and his aseity. He does this, in part, by arguing for what he thinks are other absolute necessities alongside God. For example, he argues that while the redness of a rose may be within God's control, the proposition "whatever is red is colored" is not within his control. This latter proposition is a necessary truth, and necessary truths, according to Plantinga, are not up to God; they are true by virtue of what they are. If they were within God's control, according to Plantinga, then God could cause them to be false. In other words, if they were within God's control, they would have to be contingent truths. But God could not cause such propositions to be false, since they are true necessarily.

What does this have to do with the doctrine of divine simplicity? Simplicity requires that there is nothing on which God is essentially dependent. If there were, then God would only be "potential" with respect to what he is, rather than essentially actual. In other words, he would not be who he is unless other things were true and applied to him; he would be potentially something or someone else. If it can be shown that there are some things on which God is dependent necessarily, then it should not be difficult for us to affirm that there are other things, things that compose who God is, on which he is dependent as well. So (to oversimplify), Plantinga's argument here is that since

---

80. Ibid., 229.

God is dependent on a number of things, we should have no problem rejecting the notion of simplicity.[81]

There are other, much more detailed arguments offered by Plantinga, but this will have to do for now. In response to his discussion, we could ask, first, is it really the case that if God is identical with his properties, then there is only one property, and God is in fact a property? Perhaps that follows logically (given a certain understanding of "property"), but there are other ways to construe the relationship.

We should remember here that we are discussing apophatic theology. That is, we are focusing on what God is not. The doctrine of divine simplicity affirms that there are certain ways in which we are not to think of God. For example, we are not to think that God is made up of a number of parts. So, in arguments for simplicity, we are not saying that God is unqualifiedly identical with his attributes.

Rather, the argument for simplicity must include our understanding of the Trinity. While we affirm the oneness of God, we must also note real distinctions in him that are not in any way different from who he essentially is. In other words, simplicity affirms no composition in God, but it also affirms *real* (though not *essential*) distinctions in God (who is *really* Father, Son, and Holy Spirit). The same is true for God's attributes, or properties. Goodness is not, first of all, a property of God's that we deem identical with him; goodness is who God, the personal God, *is*. Its status as a property is only secondary to its status as God. So also for the other attributes.

We should also see that, to construe the argument differently, if God is identical with his properties, it may be (and in fact is the case) that, rather than God being a property, the property is

---

81. We should remember here that the rejection of simplicity is common among evangelical theologians. If, as many of them affirm, God gives up his sovereignty in order for us to be truly free, then it is a very short step to a dependent (open?) God.

first of all a tripersonal property. Since, historically, a property has been considered a "mode" and not a "thing," it requires some essential thing in order to exist at all; it cannot exist without something essential grounding its existence. So, God's properties are both distinct and identical with him. He alone is substantial or essential; his properties are not substantial, in that sense, but are modal, and are modally related to the personal distinctions in the Godhead.[82]

The other reason Plantinga wants to force the identity in the direction of properties is that he is convinced that at least some properties are necessarily what they are, whether or not God exists. So, conceptual priority is given to properties, rather than to God, at the outset. This priority, however, gets things backwards. If we begin our reasoning with God as *a se*, then we should recognize that, before God created, there was only the triune God. There were no necessities, no properties at all that, along with God, were not themselves identical to him. Thus, for example, before the foundation of the world, there were no

---

Plantinga, generally, falls into this category. His free-will defense is basically Arminian, so he should have no problem rejecting simplicity on the same grounds. For a summary and analysis of Plantinga's free-will defense, see K. Scott Oliphint, *Reasons for Faith: Philosophy in the Service of Theology* (Phillipsburg, NJ: P&R Publishing, 2006), part 4.

82. A crucial point related to this, which cannot be developed here, is that this *modal* distinction also helps us see how there are distinct attributes in a simple God. According to Charles Hodge, "The divine attributes differ . . . *virtualiter*. If this be understood to mean that the divine perfections are really what the Bible declares them to be; *that God truly thinks, feels, and acts; that He is truly wise, just, and good; that He is truly omnipotent, and voluntary, acting or not acting, as He sees fit; that He can hear and answer prayer; it may be admitted.* But we are not to give up the conviction that God is really in Himself what He reveals Himself to be, to satisfy any metaphysical speculations as to the difference between essence and attribute in an infinite Being. The attributes of God, therefore, are not merely different conceptions in our minds, but *different modes* in which God reveals Himself to his creatures (or to Himself)." Charles Hodge, *Systematic Theology* (Oak Harbor, WA: Logos Research Systems, 1997), 1:373–74 (emphases added).

necessary propositions that *had to* obtain, since there were no propositions at all. There was only God—Father, Son, and Holy Spirit—the one God. There was no "2 + 2 = 4," no "all things red are colored"; there was only God and his triune, essential character—nothing else.

This brings us to the second response, a response to Plantinga's rejection of the SAI. Is it really the case that, since the proposition "whatever is red is colored" is a necessary truth, God has no control over it? Or, to use a more abstract example, is it the case that since two plus two equals four necessarily, God has no control over it? Must it be that to acknowledge God's control over it means that it must be possible for God to make it false? These questions are integrally related to current discussions of possible worlds and of modal logic and cannot be dealt with in depth here. We can say, however, that the answers to these questions have everything to do with how we think of the modal notions of necessity and possibility.

How do we know, for example, that two plus two necessarily equals four? One way is to look at the meaning of the terms. Four consists necessarily of two and two. So, it simply could not be four unless two and two were included in it (in some way). But what kind of necessity is this? Is it the same necessity that we apply to God's existence? It cannot be the case that God and creation, including the necessary laws of creation, are subject to the same necessity.

A better, biblical affirmation is that necessity and possibility are all determined by God himself. This means that there is no such thing as a possible world (i.e., a possible state of affairs) in which God does not exist. Nothing else can partake of this kind of necessity. Regarding the notion of necessity, therefore, we must maintain a distinction between God's necessity and the necessity of anything else. The triune God, who alone is absolutely necessary, determines everything else that is possible and necessary.

In order to think correctly about the modal notion of necessity, we should see it as defined in one way for created things and in another way for the triune God. Whatever is necessary for us is such because God has so ordered and determined the world in that way. He might have determined it in that way because it more closely reflects something of who he is. So, for example, the reason God cannot square a circle is not that he is subject to some necessity outside himself or in some way constraining his character, but because he created a circle to be a certain way, and a square to be a certain way, and thus their necessity lies in his creative hand, not in something abstract and above God. God, then, is indeed sovereign over that which is necessary in creation, because he is the author of that necessity.

So, must we affirm that if God is in control of something, it must be possible for it to be false? There seems to be no indication that we must. God is in control of, for example, the true proposition that everyone who calls on the name of the Lord will be saved, but that does not mean that God can make that statement false. The book of Hebrews reminds us that God swore by himself that he would be true to his promises. The necessity of this truth (and others) lies in his faithful character, not in an abstract, modal notion to which he must be subject.

The same is true of all he created. Some things in creation are indeed changeable, but his creation also includes necessary elements, all of which are the way they are because of his sovereign activity, not because of a metaphysical reality (other than himself) to which he had to conform in order to create. This conditional or created necessity is what the Reformed have called "hypothetical necessity." Anything that is necessary in creation is necessary only because of God's free decision to create some things as necessary. There is a *condition* (i.e., hypothesis) attached to every created necessity.

With Plantinga's objections set aside, let us analyze Thomas's view of divine simplicity from the perspective of some of his best contemporary advocates, who recognize the persistent problems that ensue when simplicity is affirmed. Once we see what Thomas's followers see with respect to his view of simplicity, we will be able to offer a more biblical understanding of it.

Thomas Morris describes the central problems with the notion of divine simplicity like this:

> If there is no multiplicity of properties really had by God, it will, I think, be very hard, if not just impossible, to make sense of standard distinctions we make about God. We believe that he is necessarily powerful, but that it is only contingently true of him that he used that power to create our world. He could have created another universe instead, or, perhaps, he could have refrained from creating any physical realm at all. We also believe that it is only contingently, not necessarily, true of God that he called Abram out of Ur, spoke through Moses, and sent the prophets he chose.... God necessarily is a knower. God contingently has the knowledge that I have on a striped shirt. Thus, there is both necessity and contingency with respect to God. And there seems to be no other good way to capture this truth than to say that God has both necessary (essential) and contingent properties. But if that is so, then he cannot "have" just one and only one property, a single property with which he is identical.[83]

We can summarize the problems that Morris highlights under two general categories: God's freedom and his responsiveness to and in creation.

---

83. Thomas V. Morris, "Problems with Divine Simplicity," in *Philosophy of Religion: A Guide and Anthology*, ed. Brian Davies (Oxford: Oxford University Press, 2000), 548.

In her monumental and thorough exposition of Thomas Aquinas's thought, Eleonore Stump seeks to defend Thomas's notion of simplicity. She wants to affirm simplicity, not simply by explaining Thomas's view, but by highlighting and addressing the problems that attach to such a notion. She believes, as Morris highlights above, that the most perplexing problem for Thomas's view of divine simplicity finds its focus in the freedom of God (which includes his responsiveness).[84] The freedom of God extends itself into the problems of contingency in God, and of God's responsiveness to his creation and to his people, as recorded in Scripture.

Stump is rightly sensitive to these problems, and she works through the relevant texts of Aquinas in order to provide solutions. First, on contingency, Stump says,

> If we can distinguish between necessitated divine acts and divine acts such that it is possible for God to have done otherwise, in what sense is there no distinction within God? It seems, on the face of it, that this analysis attributes contingency to some of God's acts. And if some divine acts are contingent, then it seems that God does have intrinsic accidental properties, properties such that God could exist and have properties other than these, contrary to the explicit claims of the doctrine of divine simplicity.[85]

The problem of God's freedom has to do with the possibility of God having *intrinsic* accidental properties. If God has intrinsic accidental properties, then he can be changed by virtue of those properties. God can, of course, have extrinsic accidental properties, because such properties would not require a change in

---

84. Stump, *Aquinas*, 100.
85. Ibid., 108–9.

God.[86] How, then, can Thomistic simplicity extricate itself from the reality of intrinsic accidental properties as constituents of God's freedom?

In order to address this question, Stump picks out, as a paradigmatic case of contingency, God's act of creation. How can we reconcile the notion that God freely chose to create, and thus acted in a way that he did not have to act, with Thomas's doctrine of simplicity? "If God can do other than he does, then it is possible for God to exist as God and yet will differently from the way he actually does will. If the nature of God is invariable, God must be the same in all possible worlds in which he exists."[87]

Stump helpfully shows that the notion of "accident" in Thomas is not coincident with the standard modal locutions of today. She argues that Peter of Spain, for example, did not think of accidents as changes across possible worlds, but instead saw them as changes across time. So also, Thomas does not use the notion of accident in terms of "synchronous possibilities across different possible worlds. Instead, he characterizes an accident . . . as something that has being but in an incomplete sort of way."[88]

If this is the case, then the negation of accidents in God is not a negation of God's freedom—such that he must be the same in all possible worlds—but rather is a negation of anything incomplete or insubstantial in God. In this case, says Stump, being one's own nature is compatible with change across possible worlds.[89]

In sum, with respect to accidental properties and God's simplicity, Stump notes that Thomas

> does not take any property anything has in some but not all possible worlds in which it exists as an accident of that thing;

86. Ibid., 97.
87. Ibid., 111.
88. Ibid.
89. Ibid., 113. Stump references *ST*, 1a.19.3 obj. 4 and ad 4 for support.

and, on his view, a thing can be its own nature without that thing's having only properties necessary to it. . . . For him the denial that God has accidents does not entail that God is the same in all possible worlds in which he exists, and the claim that God is his own nature does not entail that God is necessarily whatever he is.[90]

But does this really provide a solution to the problem of freedom and divine simplicity? If God wills one thing contingently, does that not mean that God's will is intrinsically *distinct*, such that it cannot be one, simple will? Does that not entail that God's will is both necessary and contingent, in that it can choose one thing and not another?

Stump feels the weight of this objection and so introduces the notion of "conditional necessity" with respect to God's will. Conditional necessity includes the fact that, once God contingently chooses a particular act, say, creation, then any act contrary to that is no longer available to him. If we combine that contingent choice of God's with his eternity, then, argues Stump, the necessity of his contingent choice is analogous to the necessity of the present.[91] So God's "act of creating is a timeless action in the eternal present, and so it is logically impossible for there to be anything before (or after) his act of creating."[92]

Not only so, and this will be important below, Stump argues that this conditional necessity with respect to God's will is *not intrinsic* to his will, but is, instead, a "Cambridge property."[93] That is, the property is extrinsic to God's one will, thus having no intrinsic effect on his simple nature:

90. Ibid., 115.
91. The necessity of the present recognizes that if it is the case *now* that I am sitting here, then there is no possibility that I could be running *now* or standing *now*.
92. Stump, *Aquinas*, 123.
93. Ibid., 125.

But although the differing relationships and differing coun-terfactuals imply that God is not the same in all possible worlds, they do not show that in any given world God's act of will is not one single metaphysically indivisible act. They provide the basis for drawing a conceptual distinction among Cambridge properties of God's will, but because the distinction arises just from considering the different ways in which the divine will can be related to its objects, they do not constitute a metaphysical distinction among God's intrinsic properties.[94]

So, because God's contingent choices only produce Cambridge properties—properties extrinsic to him and thus not in any way affecting him intrinsically—the simplicity of God's will can be affirmed.

With respect to the second general conundrum of divine simplicity, that is, God's responsiveness, Stump again recognizes the seriousness of the problem for simplicity:

> If it is the case that everything that God is and does is identi-cal with his being, then God's talking to Cain is identical with his being. If God talks to Cain, then God's talking to Cain is not part of his essence; it is his essence, and God himself is that essence. Not only so, but if God's talking to Cain is essen-tial to God, then it is apparently necessary, and not something God could refrain from doing.[95]

In response to this, Stump first affirms what has been standard fare in theology proper, namely, that God wills both himself and everything else in one, eternal act of will:

94. Ibid., 126.
95. Ibid., 198.

As Aquinas understands it, God's willing himself and other things consists in God's willing at once, in one action, both goodness and the manifestation of goodness; and there is no special difficulty in understanding goodness to be manifested differently to different persons on different occasions . . . in ways that must be counted among the extrinsic accidental properties of the goodness manifested. On Aquinas's view, the multiplicity of the objects of God's will is no more in tension with his simplicity than the multitude of the objects of his knowledge is.[96]

In other words, there is no change in the will of God just because the object(s) of that one will are different. So, whatever God chooses is identical with that one will, which itself could have chosen another world or no world at all. It is God's one divine act of will, even though its objects are not the same across possible choices God could have made.

But will this explanation suffice to defend Thomas's doctrine of divine simplicity? In a fascinating and penetrating analysis of Thomas's doctrine of divine simplicity, Brian Leftow remains unconvinced that Stump has successfully defended Thomas's view. We will focus on Leftow's argument against the idea that the contingency of God's will can be an extrinsic, Cambridge property of his. According to Leftow,

A feature of Thomas' general modal metaphysics defeats the claim that what makes it the case that God's being F [for example, F = Creator] is contingent is extrinsic. Thomas holds views which imply that if there "are" possible worlds, prior to all Creation, they exist "in God's power," in the strong sense that what makes talk of them true is really God's power. God's power is intrinsic to him, then if God is contingently F

96. Ibid., 199.

[e.g., Creator], the worlds which make it the case that God's being *F* is contingent are intrinsic to God. . . . If Thomas wants to make the extrinsic-modality move, this part of his modal metaphysics stands in his way.[97]

The argument here is that since God's power is intrinsic to his nature, and since nothing can come to be without God's power, the *mode* by which anything comes to be cannot be extrinsic to God, but must be intrinsic; it must be according to, since it is based on, the intrinsic power of his simple nature.

Leftow further recognizes the difficulty with respect to the simplicity of God's will, namely, that it acts according to one, simple act. As with Stump, he focuses the discussion on the contingency of creation:

> Let's ask just how a necessarily simple event can contingently fall under the description "willing creatures to exist." This description is either intrinsic or extrinsic. If intrinsic, it can't fail to apply in virtue of a difference in part or in the broader sort of constituent a Thomist accident . . . is. A simple event is its own only constituent. Add a part or constituent and the result is not simple, and so not that event if the event is necessarily simple. Substitute something else for the one constituent the event is and the result is not that event either. But what other than a difference in part, accident or property *could* account for an intrinsic description's applying contingently?[98]

The point here is that, once the contingency of an event, say, creation, comes into view with respect to God's will, it doesn't

97. Brian Leftow, "Aquinas, Divine Simplicity and Divine Freedom," in *Metaphysics and God: Essays in Honor of Eleonore Stump*, ed. Kevin Timpe (London: Routledge, 2009), 32.

98. Ibid., 32–33.

seem possible to affirm the simplicity of God; his will is now differentiated according to what he did, but did not have to do. In other words, a *modal* distinction in the will of God between the necessary and the contingent is sufficient to undermine Thomas's view of divine simplicity. "So," says Leftow, "it seems both that 'willing creatures' must be intrinsic and that if intrinsic it can't on Thomas' terms apply contingently."[99]

Leftow then asks if the problem can be solved by an appeal to the "manner" of God's willing. By this he means the "way" or mode of God's willing. Could it be that the one, simple will of God could remain one and simple and act in a different way or manner? Leftow doesn't think so. Even if the manner is different, when the will is one and simple, there is still some real distinction intrinsic to God:

> If the same event could have taken place in a different manner, one could have the event without the manner. So event and manner can't be just identical, it seems. So mustn't there be some real distinction in God between the willing and the manner, and how is this compatible with divine simplicity? There either is or is not something in which it consists for the willing to be in the one manner or the other. If there is, it seems that that something must be there contingently and so we introduce internal complexity in a simple God. If there is not, we are no better off than we were with Stump's simple solution: we seem to solve the problem by magic.[100]

As we pointed out above, Stump is well aware of the problems for Thomas's view of divine simplicity that Leftow highlights. As she noted, the contingency of God's will (with

99. Ibid., 33.
100. Ibid., 36.

the attendant problem of God's responsiveness) is *the* conundrum when the notion of divine simplicity is affirmed. Just how could one move from simplicity to the contingent acts of God's one, simple will?

In a later article on simplicity, Stump reexamines and rethinks her previous exposition of Thomas's doctrine of divine simplicity.[101] In the context of her reexamination, Stump offers a new way to consider Thomas's view. She argues for what she calls "quantum metaphysics"—which, she thinks, fits more closely with the overall emphases of Thomas's philosophical theology, and which helps to better explain his doctrine of divine simplicity. In this article, Stump moves much closer to what a biblical view of God's simplicity would require. In order to move our discussion in that direction, we will summarize her exposition of divine simplicity as she employs Thomas's categories of God's *esse* and his *id quod est*.[102]

Stump argues that we can better understand divine simplicity when we recognize Thomas's distinction, use, and application of God's *esse* (being) and his *id quod est* (essence). We cannot focus only on God's being (*esse*), says Stump, when discussing Thomas's notion of simplicity. We must always include as well the essence (*id quod est*) of God. For Thomas, as we have seen, these two are identical in God. In him alone are being and essence identical. God does not exist (*esse*) *with* a nature (*id quod est*); he *is* (*esse*) that nature (*id quod est*). This does not mean, however, for Thomas, that there is no *distinction* to be made between God's *esse* and his *id quod est*. And with this distinction, Stump thinks

101. Eleonore Stump, "God's Simplicity," in *The Oxford Handbook of Aquinas*, ed. Brian Davies and Eleonore Stump (New York: Oxford University Press, 2012), 135–46. There is no indication in this article that Stump is responding specifically to Leftow's analysis of divine simplicity. Her response does, however, apply to that analysis, even if inadvertently.

102. Because Stump chooses, in the interest of maximal clarity, to use the Latin phrases, we will do so as well. See ibid., 137.

she has a better, richer way to articulate Aquinas's view of God's simplicity.

In her analysis, Stump recognizes that any view of God as *esse* alone, and not also as *id quod est*, has the advantage of overcoming the conundrums above with respect to Thomas's view of divine simplicity. Anything that is not an *id quod est* has no accidental or contingent properties. In other words, if *esse* signifies nothing concrete (as *id quod est* does), then anything that is only *esse* can have no concrete properties at all. Stump uses the example of whiteness: "Whiteness does not have a certain size or quantity, for example; it does not engage in action or receive the action of anything else. . . . *Whiteness* is what it is—whiteness—and nothing else at all."[103] But it cannot be the case, Stump argues, that, for Thomas, God is only *esse*:

> In my view, the problem with this interpretation is not that it identifies God with *esse*. The problem is that it rejects the notion of God as *id quod est*. This rejection looks sensible, especially given Aquinas's care to distinguish *esse* from *id quod est*; but, in fact, it is not true to Aquinas's position.[104]

For Aquinas, God is both *esse* and *id quod est*. "In simple things, *esse* itself and *id quod est* must be one and the same as regards the things themselves (*realiter*)."[105]

But, given Thomas's distinction between an *esse* and an *id quod est*—where the former is always and only abstract and the latter is always and only concrete—it may appear that "Aquinas

---

103. Ibid., 138. It is worth noting that Stump sees striking parallels between this understanding of God's simplicity as *esse* only and Plantinga's construal of Thomas's doctrine of divine simplicity, in that Plantinga denies Thomistic simplicity because it cannot allow for God as *personal*.

104. Ibid., 139.

105. Ibid., 140, quoting Thomas's commentary on Boethius's *De hebdomanibus*.

is willing to violate the laws of logic as regards God."[106] He is positing that two incompatible properties are actually identical. It cannot be the case, however, that this is a violation of logic, as Thomas makes clear elsewhere. It is at this point that Stump invokes the notion of quantum metaphysics:

> What kind of thing is it that has to be understood both as a wave and as a particle? We do not know. That is, we do not know the *quid est* of light. . . . Analogously, we can ask: What kind of thing is it that can be both *esse* and *id quod est*? We do not know. The idea of simplicity is that at the ultimate *metaphysical* foundation of reality is something that has to be understood as *esse*—but also as *id quod est*. We do not know what kind of thing this is either. And this conclusion is precisely what we should expect from Aquinas's insistence that we do not know the *quid est* of God.[107]

Stump goes on to affirm that, for Aquinas, this does not mean that we can have no positive knowledge of God. As with light, there are true affirmations that quantum physics is able to recognize; so also with God.

"For this reason," says Stump, "we have to exercise care in the way we frame our claims about God. It is acceptable to say that God is *esse*, provided that we understand that this claim does not rule out the equally true claim that God is *id quod est*, an entity, a concrete particular."[108]

With this, in our estimation, Stump begins to move much closer to a biblical, revelational understanding of God's simplicity. In affirming Thomas's view of simplicity, Stump is arguing,

---

106. Ibid.
107. Ibid.
108. Ibid., 141.

we cannot be content simply with affirming the "being" (*esse*) of God. Those who emphasize only *esse* not only fall prey to Plantinga's critique, but also "can leave one with the impression that the immutable, impassible, eternal, simple God of Thomistic philosophical theology is frozen, static, inert, unresponsive, and incapable of action."[109]

How is it, then, that this simple God is capable of action, all the while remaining simple?

> The doctrine of simplicity implies that at the ultimate meta-physical foundation of all reality there is *esse*. But it also implies that this *esse, without losing any of its characteristics* as *esse, is something subsistent* and concrete, with more ability to act and with more freedom in its acts than any concrete com-posite entity has.[110]

The advantage, then, of a "quantum metaphysics" view of divine simplicity is that we can now characterize God in terms of those attributes that accrue to his oneness—attributes such as eternity and immutability—and we can also characterize him as the one who *acts*, without in any way undermining or negating his essential character. To use Stump's example, "Sometimes we have to characterize God with abstract terms—and so we say that God is love—and sometimes we have to characterize him with concrete terms—and so we say that God is loving."[111]

So, even though we have no way of knowing how such

---

109. Ibid., 142. This "impression" is not without its advocates in Thomism. In a current book on divine simplicity, for example, Paul Hinlicky sees this "frozen" view of God's simplicity—"protological simplicity" as he calls it—as originating from a Thomistic understanding of God. Hinlicky's analysis of at least some Thomists is accurate, though his solutions are seriously wanting. See Paul R. Hinlicky, *Divine Simplicity: Christ the Crisis of Metaphysics* (Grand Rapids: Baker Academic, 2016).

110. Stump, "God's Simplicity," 142 (emphases added).

111. Ibid., 141.

apparently incompatible aspects of God's character can cohere, we can, and must, affirm them both. As Stump concludes, "To try to explain the doctrine of simplicity in this way is not to provide an argument for the truth or even the compatibility of its claims."[112]

We have belabored these significant and substantial discussions of Thomas's view of divine simplicity because they begin to move us, inexorably, toward a biblical view of God's simplicity. Now that the issues are before us, we can broach a more robustly revelational solution to the conundrums that divine simplicity entails.

What is most helpful about the distinction between *esse and id quod est* is that it points us to the relationship between God's one essence and his tripersonal character. Stump recognizes that if God is *esse* only (as Plantinga seems to imply), then there would be no way in which God could be personal: "Nothing that is not an *id quod est* could be a person or enter into personal relationship with human persons."[113]

If we begin with biblical revelation, however (something that Thomas's natural theology cannot do) we can begin with, instead of the categories of *esse* and *id quod est*, the one *essence* of God as three *hypostases*, or *subsistences*. In other words, we can begin, contrary to Aquinas, with the ontological Trinity. With these biblical categories in view, we are able to affirm *both* that God's *essence* is who he is and that there is no possibility that he could be otherwise, *and* that each of the three *subsistences* of the Godhead can and does *act as that one essence*.

With respect to God's intrinsic character, his *esse*, the divine *persons* (in the technical sense of person as subsistence, or

---

112. Ibid., 143.
113. Ibid., 139. Despite mentioning "a person," Stump does not address the question of unipersonality, i.e., the question whether God is one person.

hypostasis) act relative to each other: the Father *begets* the Son, and the Father and the Son *spirate* the Spirit. These *ad intra*, or intrinsic, *acts* of God pertain to the persons, each of whom is himself the one God. Thus, God's simplicity, by definition, includes *ad intra* modal (or subsistent) distinctions—of Father, Son, and Holy Spirit—as well as the *ad intra* acts of God. This, indeed, might be analogous to quantum metaphysics, in which we affirm of God two or more characteristics that appear to be incompatible. But no such incompatibility exists within the triune God. There is simply no possibility that God could be in conflict with his own triune being.

With respect to the knotty problem of God's triune simplicity and his free, contingent acts of will, we must refer, in the first place, to his eternal decree, including the *pactum salutis* (covenant of redemption).[114] In this way, we would propose that the biblical notion of covenant helps us to think and speak of God's absolute, simple essence properly, with respect both to his freedom and to his responsiveness.

In the *pactum salutis*, the three persons of the Trinity are in view at the eternal point at which they determine to create and to redeem. We cannot develop this in any detail, so we will only give brief examples.

We see, for example, that the second person of the Trinity, the Son of God, "was foreknown before the foundation of the world" (1 Peter 1:20). This foreknowledge can be none other than the Father's loving of the Son "before the foundation of the world," of which Christ spoke to his disciples before his death (John 17:24). This foreknowing cannot be God's omniscience, because it has a particular, redemptive purpose in view; nor can the Father's love for the Son be the ontological love of the triune

---

114. The *pactum salutis* refers to the eternal covenant of redemption that the Father, the Son, and the Holy Spirit enacted prior to the creation of the world.

God, for the same reason: because redemption is in view. Rather, it is the love that has in view the glorified Savior, once his work on earth is finished.[115]

Not only so, but with respect to the Son, we learn that he "did not count equality with God a thing to be grasped" (Phil. 2:6). When might this consideration have occurred in the Son? It could not have been during his incarnation, because it preceded his self-emptying (v. 7). Instead, the Son, in eternity, willingly let go of his glory by taking on a human nature. This must refer to the counsel within the triune God in eternity past, the *pactum salutis*.

In this way, we can begin to see *that* (though we can never penetrate to the *how*) the one God remains who he is even while the three counsel together to will and to act according to their own respective persons. The three are *essentially* one, simple and absolute, even as they are *hypostatically* acting relative to their respective, personal modes of subsistence. In the *pactum salutis*, according to Geerhardus Vos, there is one divine will, but:

> *This will appears as having its own mode of existence in each person.* One cannot object to this on the basis of the unity of God's being. To push unity so strongly that the persons can no longer be related to one another judicially would lead to Sabellianism and would undermine the reality of the entire economy of redemption with its person to person relationships.[116]

---

115. For an elaboration of this point, see K. Scott Oliphint, *The Majesty of Mystery: Celebrating the Glory of an Incomprehensible God* (Bellingham, WA: Lexham Press, 2016), ch. 6.

116. Geerhardus Vos, "The Doctrine of the Covenant in Reformed Theology," in *Redemptive History and Biblical Interpretation: The Shorter Writings of Geerhardus Vos*, ed. Richard B. Gaffin Jr. (Phillipsburg, NJ: Presbyterian and Reformed, 1980), 246 (emphasis added).

More specifically, John Owen relates the being or *essence* of God to the subsistent *acts* of God this way:

> Such is the distinction of the persons in the unity of the divine essence, as that they act in natural and essential acts *reciprocally* one towards another,—namely, in understanding, love, and the like; they know and mutually love each other. And as they subsist distinctly, so they also act distinctly in those works which are of external operation. And whereas all these acts and operations, whether reciprocal [i.e., *ad intra* or intrinsic] or external [i.e., *ad extra* or extrinsic], are either with a will or from a freedom of will and choice, the will of God in each person, as to the peculiar acts ascribed unto him, is his will therein peculiarly and eminently, though not exclusively to the other persons, by reason of their mutual *in-being*. The will of God as to the peculiar actings of the Father in this matter is the will of the Father, and the will of God with regard unto the peculiar actings of the Son is the will of the Son; *not by a distinction of sundry wills, but by the distinct application of the same will unto its distinct acts in the persons of the Father and the Son.* And in this respect the covenant [i.e., *pactum salutis*] whereof we treat differeth from a pure decree; for from these distinct actings of the will of God in the Father and the Son there doth arise a new habitude or relation, which is not natural or necessary unto them, but freely taken on them.[117]

We can begin to see here how a *triune* notion of simplicity is the only proper way to accommodate the language that Stump is concerned to maintain. God is love with respect to his essential

---

117. John Owen, *An Exposition of the Epistle to the Hebrews*, in *The Works of John Owen*, ed. W. H. Goold (Edinburgh: T. & T. Clark, 1862), 19:87–88 (emphases added).

being; that *love* of God (*esse*), to use Stump's example, is *loving* with respect to the distinct and respective *acts* of the persons of the Godhead. This emphasis moves us from a rather amorphous idea of God's *id quod est* to the necessarily *personal* character of that which is "concrete" in God. In other words, when the question is asked as to *what kind* of *esse* God is, the first answer should be that he is a *triune personal esse*. And here we begin to highlight again the traditional, Reformed understanding of the mutual interdependence of Trinity and simplicity.[118]

Stump makes the point that the properties of one mind and will of God refer us to his *id quod est*. That could be right, but we must also recognize that the willing and knowledge of God, all the while remaining essentially one, is also hypostatically and really distinct in each of the persons of the Trinity. God's one will distinctly acts and operates according to the Three.

Thus, the more helpful, biblical distinction is not that between *esse* and *id quod est*; these categories are all that is available according to natural reason. Rather, the biblical-theological categories are the standard ones highlighting God's one essence as three persons. These categories alone can provide a proper understanding of what we mean when we ascribe simplicity to God. It is simplicity with real distinctions. To paraphrase the Athanasian Creed, "The Father is simple, the Son is simple, and the Holy Spirit is simple; yet there are not three simples, but one."

There is another advantage in recognizing God's simplicity in light of the ontological Trinity. We noted above the conundrums present when different *modes* (or manners, as Leftow has it) are seen to be intrinsic to God's essential character. That is, once the

---

118. See, for example, Richard A. Muller, *Post-Reformation Reformed Dogmatics*, 3:279–93: "In this, the Reformed rejected any notion of 'absolute simplicity' in God, if that simplicity required the lack of real (though not substantial) distinctions in God."

mode of contingency is recognized in God's will, it is difficult to maintain Thomas's view of divine simplicity.

But when we see simplicity in the light of the ontological Trinity, we recognize that there are three *ad intra* persons, who are themselves distinct subsistences, *ad intra*. Those subsistences, far from undermining or denying the simplicity of God, are intrinsic to our understanding of God (including his simplicity), according to his revelation. So, we confess the simplicity of God as necessarily including three distinct and real (though not substantial) *ad intra modes* of existence in the Father, the Son, and the Holy Spirit. Surely if God's simplicity must include distinct *modes* of existence—modes that are really distinct and not just rationally attributed—then other modes necessary to God's character in no way undermine or negate his simplicity.

Add to this the proper recognition that anything contingent with respect to God must always refer to that which is *ad extra*, and we see that the Christian God, who (unlike the god of Islam, for example) is not a prisoner of his simplicity, can choose to do that which he does not have to do, and not to do that which he could do. This kind of choosing, while perhaps uncomfortable for an abstract notion of *esse* according to natural reason, is intrinsic to what it means to be a person (in the ontological sense) in the Godhead. This is quantum metaphysics in all of its biblical glory. That is to say, whenever we recognize that God is one in essence and three in persons, we will inevitably run up against notions and ideas that do not easily go together in our minds. Like quantum metaphysics, both things must be affirmed as true, even though we are not able to establish the details of the truths we affirm. Such is the case when we are thinking about a triune God who is incomprehensible.

The second conundrum that Stump seeks to solve is God's *responsiveness*. How can it be, to use Stump's example, that God can talk to Cain at one moment in history and not talk to him at another, if God is simple? Here again, the biblical notion of covenant is equipped to explain this.

We can illustrate this by focusing on God's climactic and quintessential responsiveness to creation in the Son, specifically in the incarnation.[119] Though there is much to say about this, we will confine ourselves to the specific matter at hand.[120]

How are we to think of the incarnation with respect to the *esse* of God and his *id quod est*? Better, how must we think of God becoming man when we consider who he is essentially and who he is personally? The easy part of the answer is that "God becoming man" relates only to the second person of the Trinity. But what does this "becoming" mean with respect to the essence of God?

It might help to think of it this way, and here we are indebted to Herman Bavinck. Bavinck notes that "God's *trinitarian* [i.e., *personal*] essence is the presupposition and condition of the incarnation of God." By that he means to say, "Not the divine nature as such but specifically the person of the Son became [man]."[121] In other words, the reason we can acknowledge the *relative* human nature of the Son, is that, *as Son*, he is *relatively* distinct from the other persons *ad intra*, even while he is *essentially* identical to them, that essence itself being simple (and immutable, etc.). To put it another way, Bavinck says,

119. We should mention here Stump's enlightening and helpful chapter 14 on "The Metaphysics of the Incarnation," in Stump, *Aquinas*, 407–26.

120. For a fuller development of this, see K. Scott Oliphint, *God with Us*, rev. ed. (forthcoming).

121. Herman Bavinck, *Reformed Dogmatics*, vol. 3, *Sin and Salvation in Christ*, ed. John Bolt, trans. John Vriend (Grand Rapids: Baker Academic, 2006), 275. Note the original: "Van belang is het daarom ook vast te houden, dat niet de Goddelijke natuur als zoodanig, maar bepaald—*de Persoon des Zoons mensch is geworden*." Herman Bavinck, *Gereformeerde Dogmatiek* (Kampen: J. H. Kok, 1967), 3:254 (emphasis added). The translation from the Dutch should have read, not that the Son "became a human," as in the published translation, but that he "became man." Theologically speaking, "becoming a human" negates, as it does not adequately reference, the

> But Reformed theology stressed that it was the person of the
> Son who became flesh—not the substance (the underlying
> reality) [*esse*] but the subsistence (the particular being) [the
> *id quod est*] of the Son assumed our nature. The unity of the
> two natures, despite the sharp distinction between them, is
> *unalterably anchored in the person.*[122]

With this, we have the biblical application of quantum metaphysics with respect to God's responsiveness to man.

To describe the incarnation this way is not to pretend to
comprehend it; that is altogether impossible for human creatures. But it does allow us, biblically, to affirm what orthodox
theology has always affirmed concerning the one God: that he
is simple, immutable, impassible, infinite, eternal, etc.—and that,
with respect to his personal subsistences, *ad intra* modal distinctions can obtain, even when the persons are directed toward
an *ad extra* willing of God. The Son of God, in taking a human
nature, in no way became less than the one God; such a thing
is not even possible, in that God cannot deny himself (2 Tim.
2:13). He is and always remains, as God, simple, immutable,
impassible, infinite, eternal, etc. But, his mode of subsisting *ad
extra* did change, in that he took to himself, from the time of the
incarnation and into eternity, a human nature. Thus, the Son of
God, from that point forward, will always be the one God who
is personally (subsistently) united to a human nature, even as he
is and always will be *essentially* the same immutable, one God.

This, we should note, is what God's "condescension" is in
Scripture. His condescension does not and cannot change the
essential character, the *esse*, of the one God. As in the incarnation, the *essence* of the Son does not take a human nature; the

---

necessary, biblical parallels between *the man* Adam and *the man* Christ.

122. Bavinck, *Reformed Dogmatics*, 3:259 (emphases added).

person of the Son does. From the eternal decree to eternity future, God's (covenantal) condescension consists of the *persons* (which are *ad intra* modes, subsistences) expressing who God is, in their own distinctive ways, in the context of his creation. Those expressions require contingent *modes* of revelation, so that God's human creatures can know him and have fellowship with him, according to their human capacity. This is what it means for God to "come down." It is what all of history points to, so that, in the end, "the dwelling place of God is with man" (Rev. 21:3—not that the dwelling place of man is with God).

If we recognize that the incarnation is the climax, though not the first moment, of God's responsiveness to man, then we have, in redemptive history, a proper understanding of the simple and one God interacting with, and responding to, his human creatures, always through the three persons, though focally and climactically through the Son. Charles Hodge, in his comments on 1 Corinthians 10:4, puts it this way:

> This passage distinctly asserts not only the preëxistence of our Lord, but also that *he was the Jehovah of the Old Testament*. He who appeared to Moses and announced himself as Jehovah, the God of Abraham, who commissioned him to go to Pharaoh, who delivered the people out of Egypt, who appeared on Horeb, who led the people through the wilderness, who dwelt in the temple, who manifested himself to Isaiah, who was to appear personally in the fulness of time, is the person who was born of a virgin, and manifested himself in the flesh. He is called, therefore, in the Old Testament, an angel, the angel of Jehovah, Jehovah, the Supreme Lord, the Mighty God, the Son of God—one whom God sent—one with him, therefore, as to substance, but a distinct person.[123]

123. Charles Hodge, *An Exposition of the First Epistle to the Corinthians* (New York:

Geerhardus Vos is eloquent in his assessment of the Son in the Old Testament:

> Sacramental condescensions on God's part include his appearing in human/visible form. . . . Behind the Angel speaking as God, and who embodied in Himself all the condescension of God to meet the frailty and limitations of man, there existed at the same time another aspect of God, in which he could not be seen and materially received after such a fashion, the very God of whom the Angel spoke in the third person. In the incarnation of our Lord we have the supreme expression of this fundamental arrangement. *The form in which the Angel appeared was a form assumed for the moment,* laid aside again as soon as the purpose of its assumption had been served.[124]

Once we recognize the biblical category of covenant, in which the triune God expresses himself *ad extra* with respect to creation, we also recognize that such expressions of God are always personal and that they do not, because they cannot, in any way affect or alter his simple, divine essence. Instead, the persons express themselves in relative and contingent ways (e.g., grace, wrath, jealousy, mercy, etc.), so that we might know and have fellowship with him.

It is certainly the case that Thomas's doctrine of the Trinity can be consulted with some profit with respect to what these relations are in the Godhead.[125] The problem, however, as we

---

Robert Carter & Brothers, 1857), 175 (emphasis added).

124. Taken from the discussion of the "Angel of the Lord" in Geerhardus Vos, *Biblical Theology, Old and New Testaments* (Grand Rapids: Eerdmans, 1948), 72, 74 (emphasis added). For more on the importance of the Son's activity throughout redemptive history, see K. Scott Oliphint, *God with Us,* rev. ed. (forthcoming).

125. But note Muller: "The Reformers tended not only to defend the traditional doctrine of the Trinity as biblical but also to deemphasize the authority of

have demonstrated above, is that his *principia* would not permit such a robust exposition to directly affect his affirmation and exposition of God's simplicity; that exposition was confined to natural theology and thus to natural reason. That is what happens when a revelational *principium* does not inform theology at the outset. As Thomas himself said, "A small error at the beginning of something is a great one at the end."[126] An error in *principium*, however, is anything but small. It influences more or less everything else that is said from that point forward.[127]

---

the traditional trinitarian terminology—particularly the *more speculative language of the medieval scholastics concerning the character of the trinitarian emanations in the Godhead.*" Richard A. Muller, *Post-Reformation Reformed Dogmatics: The Rise and Development of Reformed Orthodoxy, ca. 1520 to ca. 1725*, vol. 4, *The Triunity of God* (Grand Rapids: Baker Academic, 2003), 151 (emphasis added).

126. Aquinas, "On Being and Essence," 33.

127. For more on the relationship of Thomas's *principium* to his theology, see K. Scott Oliphint, "Aquinas: A Shaky Foundation," Nov. 7, 2012, https://www.thegospelcoalition.org/article/aquinas-a-shaky-foundation.

4

CONCLUSION

There is much that could be said about the thought and theology of Thomas Aquinas that has not been broached in this short study. We have had to be highly selective in our analysis. Whatever else is said, however, must take into account the methodological problems that underlie everything that Thomas wrote. Perhaps his claim at the end of his life that all he had written was of such "little value" was due, not to a "mystical experience," but to the realization of his principial error from the beginning of his work. Perhaps not. Even if not, the value of reading Thomas—which is significant in terms of its historical and theological impact—must always be measured against this initial, seminal, foundational, theological misstep.[1]

We should reiterate here again that, from our perspective, McInerny's analysis and reaffirmation of Thomas's commitment to natural reason and its *praeambula fidei* certainly fits with centuries of the Roman Catholic tradition, all told.

---

1. It is worth noting that, according to Swafford, de Lubac held that both views are in Aquinas and that it is not clear which one is predominant. For more on this, see Andrew Dean Swafford, *Nature and Grace: A New Approach to Thomistic*

Nonetheless, confusion remains in that debate. However, even if the "new" interpretation of Thomas is correct, there is no escaping his commitment to the neutrality of reason. And it is that commitment that allows for an incompatibility of the philosophical with the theological in his *principia*, which renders them impossible to merge. It is also the case, we should recognize, that these incompatible ideas are adopted in Arminian theology.[2]

For some, perhaps many, Thomists, it might appear strange that our critique of Thomas focused, in part, on an exegesis of Scripture, for whatever his strength were, he was no exegete. The point of that focus was twofold: First, it was important to see how Thomas's understanding of some key passages—passages that outline a revelational epistemology—were read by him. Because Thomas was convinced that the philosophers were able, without special revelation, to come to some genuine knowledge about God by way of demonstration, his reading of "the light" in John 1 and of "the truth" in Romans 1 was informed by philosophical, rather than exegetical, considerations.

Second, it was important to recognize that a Reformed critique of Thomas's epistemology—his *principium cognoscendi*—had to begin, not with *philosophy*, but with Scripture. Thomas was, as we have said, a man of his time. But he had the same Scriptures available to him that the church has had for two

---

Ressourcement (Eugene, OR: Pickwick Publications, 2014), 77.

2. Some evangelicals, however, have noted the inconsistency of adopting Thomas's *principia* and rejecting the rest of his theology. In that sense, Arminian or evangelical theology is a subset of Romanist theology. Certainly for Thomas, his *principia* are consistent with his Romanist theology. For the similarities and differences between Arminian and Romanist theology, see Douglas M. Beaumont, ed., *Evangelical Exodus: Evangelical Seminarians and Their Paths to Rome* (Ignatius Press, 2016). See my review in *Themelios* 41, 2 (August 2016), http://themelios.thegospelcoalition .org/review/evangelical-exodus-evangelical-seminarians-and-their-paths-to-rome. Beaumont argues that Aquinas's plea for a trust in man's natural reason leads consistently to ultimate trust in the Roman church, and not in Scripture's own self-attesting authority.

thousand years, and therefore he could have moved his theology explicitly onto a scriptural foundation. Any critique offered of Thomas must begin where Thomas should and could have begun: with the Bible.

Even as a man of his time, Thomas had access to a better, more biblical understanding of, for example, Romans 1. John of Damascus, whom Thomas quotes, says this about our knowledge of God:

> God, however, did not leave us in absolute ignorance. For the knowledge of God's existence has been implanted by Him in all by nature. This creation, too, and its maintenance, and its government, proclaim the majesty of the Divine nature. . . . That there is a God, then, is no matter of doubt to those who receive the Holy Scriptures, the Old Testament, I mean, and the New; nor indeed to most of the Greeks. For, as we said, the knowledge of the existence of God is implanted in us by nature. But . . . the wickedness of the Evil One has prevailed so mightily against man's nature as even to drive some into denying the existence of God, that most foolish and woefulest pit of destruction.[3]

It is this very passage that Thomas cites in his argument against the self-evidence of God. In his first objection, he says:

> *Objection* 1. It seems that the existence of God is self-evident. Now those things are said to be self-evident to us the knowledge of which is naturally implanted in us, as we can see in regard to first principles. But as Damascene says (*De Fid.*

---

3. John Damascene, "An Exact Exposition of the Orthodox Faith," in *St. Hilary of Poitiers, John of Damascus*, ed. Philip Schaff and Henry Wace, trans. S. D. F. Salmond, A Select Library of the Nicene and Post-Nicene Fathers of the Christian Church, Second Series, vol. 9 (New York: Christian Literature Company, 1899), 1, 3.

Orth. i. 1, 3), *the knowledge of God is naturally implanted in all.* Therefore the existence of God is self-evident.[4]

Thomas is clearly aware of the teaching of John of Damascus. He could have seen its cogency, had he looked more carefully at Romans 1:18–32 and John 1:1–9. Instead, his response to him is this:

> *Reply Obj.* 1. To know that God exists in a general and confused way is implanted in us by nature, inasmuch as God is man's beatitude. For man naturally desires happiness, and what is naturally desired by man must be naturally known to him. This, however, is not to know absolutely that God exists; just as to know that someone is approaching is not the same as to know that Peter is approaching, even though it is Peter who is approaching; for many there are who imagine that man's perfect good which is happiness, consists in riches, and others in pleasures, and others in something else.[5]

This response shows Thomas's neglect of a close, exegetical look at passages that are crucial for understanding how we know God, which was of primary concern for him. It also shows, as we noted above, Thomas's weak view of sin and its devastating effects in us.

It is impossible to know how Thomas might have reacted if he had been born in the sixteenth rather than the thirteenth century. Would he have been a proponent of the Reformation? Perhaps. But his knowledge and rejection of the Damascene's point calls seriously into question Thomas's biblical instincts. The confusion of Thomas's *principia* is owing, not centrally to

---

4. Aquinas, *ST*, I q.2 a.1 obj. 1.
5. Ibid., I q.2 a.1 ad 1.

his historical context, but centrally to his decision to try to synthesize "purely" philosophical with theological *principia*. The two *principia* cannot be merged.

This is why, with respect to the ways in which Thomas sets forth the knowledge and character of God, confusion reigns. If one reads Thomas from a Christian standpoint, then the terms and concepts that he employs can look familiar. If Thomas had begun forthrightly and explicitly from a Christian standpoint, his natural theology would have had a revelational foundation, instead of a foundation in natural reason. But reading Thomas from a Christian standpoint, in his natural theology, is to misread him; it cannot produce what Thomas wanted.

And because Thomas did not begin from a self-consciously Christian standpoint, what he wanted to argue in his natural theology cannot be sustained. Even such a devoted disciple as Cardinal Cajetan recognized that the best that Thomas's proofs could produce were concepts that *could* apply to God; they did not prove the existence of the Christian God.

So also for Thomas's natural theology proper. There are concepts and terms with which orthodox Christians can agree. Surely, God is simple, eternal, immutable, impassable, etc. The problem, however, is that there are no categories available to natural reason that can establish that these are characteristics of the Christian God.

Hume's radical empiricism showed the emptiness of dogmatic metaphysical assertions, and Kant's "corrective" to Hume demonstrated exactly how such emptiness should be articulated (i.e., as *noumenon*). Of course, Thomas had no access to these philosophers. But he too easily conceded that the "absolutes" of Greek philosophy were coincident with the Christian God. In that concession, he lost the Christian God altogether and was left with concepts just as useless as theirs.

There are other important confusions in Thomas. The most

sophisticated, thorough, and theologically articulate view of (what we now call) an Arminian approach to God's sovereignty in relation to human responsibility came from the Thomist Luis de Molina (1535–1600) and his view of *scientia media*. Molina was a committed Thomist, and he worked out much of his theology as an exposition and commentary on the First Part of the *Summa theologica*, question 14, article 13, "Whether the knowledge of God is of future contingent things?" (*Utrum scientia Dei sit futurorum contingentium*). After significant debate between the Bañezians, who denied the conditionality of God's foreknowledge,[6] and the Molinists on Thomas's view of God's foreknowledge, the Roman church tried, in earnest, to resolve the issue. They discussed the two predominant views at eighty-five different conferences in the presence of the popes, from roughly 1587 to around 1607. But the issue was never resolved in the Roman church; both sides continued to hold their respective views.[7]

It is fair to say, however, that the view of *scientia media*, in that it presupposes libertarian freedom, is the predominant view both of Romanists and of Arminians. It is also fair to say that a lack of resolution of the matter exposes another serious inconsistency in Thomas with respect to the relationship between God's sovereignty and man's will. After such a strenuous effort on the part of so many Roman church leaders and popes who were committed to Thomas as the "Angelic Doctor,"[8] it is

---

6. For a Bañezian view of Thomas, see Reginald Garrigou-Lagrange, *The One God: A Commentary on the First Part of Saint Thomas' Theological Summa* (CreateSpace Independent Publishing Platform, 2012).

7. Antonio Astrain, "Congregatio de Auxiliis," *The Catholic Encyclopedia*, vol. 4 (New York: Robert Appleton Company, 1908). Available online at www.newadvent .org/cathen/04238a.htm.

8. After Thomas was canonized in the fourteenth century, he was given the title Doctor Angelicus in the fifteenth century and was declared a Doctor of the Church in the sixteenth century.

highly doubtful that a resolution to the problem can be found in Thomas.[9]

However this and other controversies surrounding Thomas's thought should be resolved, we hope to have made it clear that any adopting or adaptation of Thomas's philosophical theology must first be filtered through the biblical theology of Reformed thought. With that filter in place, there are elements of Thomas's work that could be instructive and useful, at least from a historical perspective. Even so, every word and doctrine must be read through the grid of Thomas's two ultimately incompatible *principia*—the neutrality of natural reason, on the one hand, and the truth of God's revelation, on the other.[10] These two incompatible *principia*, more than likely, contribute substantially to the confusion that remains among Thomists with respect to some of his most significant teachings.

9. For an excellent introduction to Molinism, as well as Molina's text on divine foreknowledge, see Luis de Molina, *On Divine Foreknowledge: Part IV of the Concordia*, trans. Alfred J. Freddoso (Ithaca, NY: Cornell University Press, 1988).

10. Although Christopher Hughes misconstrues Thomas in significant ways, his plea that Thomas must either give up his view of simplicity or give up his view of the Trinity recognizes, in my view, the incompatibility of Thomas's two *principia*. See Christopher Hughes, *On a Complex Theory of a Simple God: An Investigation in Aquinas' Philosophical Theology* (Ithaca, NY: Cornell University Press, 1989).

GLOSSARY

a posteriori. Literally, "from the latter"; this is inductive reasoning that moves from the effect to cause, that is, from a specific instance to a general principle. In Aquinas, this applies to proofs of the existence of God that begin with creation and then reason back to a first cause or first mover.

a priori. Literally, "from the former"; this is deductive reasoning that moves from cause to effect, that is, from a general principle to a specific instance. This is the way that Anselm developed his ontological proof of God's existence, moving from the idea of God to the existence of God.

a se. The idea that God is self-existent and completely independent. This term was used in medieval theology and philosophy to imply that God is absolutely supreme over all other beings.

accident. A property of a thing that is not part of the essence of the thing. An accident is something that can be lost or added without the thing ceasing to be what it was before. Aristotle divided accidents into these categories: quantity, action, quality, space, time, and relation.

ad intra. Literally, "internal, inward, toward the inside"; when referring to God, this describes who he is in himself.

ad extra. Literally, "external, outward, toward the outside"; when referring to God, this describes who he is as he reveals himself in history and in his works.

analogia entis. Literally, "analogy of being"; the assumption that there is a likeness between finite and infinite being. It is the basis for *a posteriori* proofs of the existence of God and is part of the discussion of the divine attributes.

analogy of intrinsic attribution. For Aquinas, God's essence and his existence are identical. However, in creation this is not the case. Therefore, the analogy between God and creation cannot be one of proportionality (i.e., God is more of a particular thing than creation). For Thomas, the basis of the analogy between God and man is not proportionality but causality. Because the definition of potential existence is that which makes a thing what it is, that which is of the essence of a thing must be possessed fully by that thing. It follows, then, for Aquinas, that existence is not intrinsic to created being and therefore must be caused by one in whom essence and existence are identical.

analogy of proper proportionality. The metaphysical notion designed to articulate the fact that being itself cannot be seen, but is "perceived" in each thing in proportion to its essence. A thing is said to "be" in proportion to its nature. Thus, the being of a man is in some sense similar to, and in some sense dissimilar to, the being of a rock. There is, then, an analogy of proper proportionality between the rock and the man.

apophatic theology. Theology done by way of negation, saying what God is not, rather than what he is.

archetypal knowledge. God's own knowledge of himself and his works, from which creaturely, ectypal knowledge of God is drawn.

being. The basic or primary element in a thing; the thing's nature, or that without which it could not be what it is; essence.

Cambridge property. A property that is extrinsic to God's one will, thus having no intrinsic effect on his simple nature.

cause. Aristotelian philosophy recognizes four kinds of causation:
- Material cause: the substance or material that constitutes an object.
- Formal cause: the pattern or blueprint that determines the resulting form.
- Efficient cause: the agency producing the result.
- Teleological cause: the end toward which the object is directed.

demonstration. For Thomas, syllogistic reasoning that proceeds from immediate principles, either straightway or through middles.

divine simplicity. The doctrine that God is not made up of parts; he is metaphysically not composite.

duplex veritatis modus. Literally, "double ways of truth"; the theory that something can be true in two ways: the first (in methodological order) includes all that can be known about God by natural reason; the second includes those divine things that can be known only by revelation. It is possible for something to be true in philosophy but false in theology, or false in philosophy but true in theology.

ectypal knowledge. The creaturely knowledge of God and his works.

esse. Literally, "to be"; the act of existing; any given thing must have an essence ("whatness") and an existence (*esse*). E.g., a human must have both humanity (the essence of a human) and actual existence (*esse*).

essence. That which is basic or primary in a thing; the thing's nature, or that without which it could not be what it is.

foundationalism. An epistemological structure in which certain immediate, or basic, propositions are affirmed as "foundational" to our knowledge; other propositions, in order to be believed, must first be demonstrated on the basis of those foundational propositions. According to foundationalism, foundational beliefs are propositions that are either common, intuitive, and immediate or inferred from immediate propositions.

genus. A class of things that share the same character, but divide into different subclasses or species.

id quod est. Literally, "that which is"; essence or nature. For Thomas, God's *id quod est* (essence, nature) and his *esse* (being, existence) are one.

immediate propositions. Propositions that are grounded metaphysically. According to Scott MacDonald, "Immediate propositions, then, are capable of being known by virtue of themselves and are, therefore, proper objects of non-derivative knowledge. But their actually being known by virtue of themselves requires that one be acquainted with the facts expressed by those propositions, which requires that one conceive the terms of those propositions."

ipsum esse subsistens. Literally, "subsistent being itself." According to Thomas, God is the only being in which there is perfect union between essence and existence. The separation of essence and existence is unnecessary because God exists in and of himself.

kinds or modes of knowledge. For Thomas, there are three kinds or modes of knowledge:

- The first is obscure and indirect, having as its objects those things which also, even if in an ambiguous and confused way, comport indirectly with aspects of God's character or of man's existence generally. Because we are creatures, and because we know that we and other things exist, we have a general knowledge of being and of the fact of creation. This is all that such an implicit knowledge can give.

- That which is gained through demonstration by way of our natural reason.
- That which comes by revelation.

metaphysics. Originally a title for those books of Aristotle that came after the Physics. It came to be understood as the branch of philosophy that deals with first principles (i.e., concepts such as being, knowing, identity, time, and space).

natural reason. The reasoning capacity of all people apart from grace or special revelation.

necessary existence. The existence of a thing that is independent of the existence of other things. That is, if nothing else existed, it would still exist.

pactum salutis. Literally, "covenant of redemption"; in Reformed theology, this is the pretemporal, intra-Trinitarian agreement between the persons of the Trinity concerning the covenant of grace and its ratification in and through the work of the incarnate Son.

praeambula fidei. Literally, "preambles of faith"; the philosophical principles thought to be necessary, foundational, or preparatory for the rationality of the Christian faith.

principia. Fundamental principles, connected to Aristotle's notion of *arche* (beginning, origin, foundation, or source).

principium cognoscendi. Literally, "foundation of knowledge." Reformed theology recognizes two sources that are *principia cognoscendi*: the *internum*, i.e., the Holy Spirit, and the *externum*, i.e., Scripture.

principium essendi. Literally, "foundation of existence"; for Thomas, arguments for God's existence and what sort of God exists. Reformed theology argues that this refers to God.

quinque viae. *Literally, "the five ways";* Thomas's ways of demonstrating the existence of God:
- Motion is only explained by an unmoved mover, a prime mover.
- A chain of effects demands a first cause.
- The world is contingent, and that demands something that has necessary existence.
- There is a gradation of value in the world, and that calls for something that is the most valuable or perfect.
- There is an orderly character to events, which demands a goal, and the existence of this goal requires a being that ordained the goal.

realism. The view that universals do indeed exist. However, for Thomas, universals exist in the mind. These universals have their foundation in the existence of particulars.

self-evidence. For Thomas, it is important to distinguish between a proposition that is self-evident in itself (*per se*) and one that is self-evident to us. He defines a self-evident proposition as one in which the predicate is, in some essential sense, contained in the subject. Thomas's example is "Man is an animal," since the notion of "animal" is necessarily included in that of "man."

sententia. Literally, "sentence, sense, meaning"; the term can indicate a sentence or conclusion concerning an issue, judgment, decision, or opinion about something. Also a series of words or a discourse having a particular meaning or significance.

teleology. The notion that things are moving toward a particular end.

Thomism. The modified Aristotelianism of Thomas Aquinas and its development particularly in the Roman Catholic tradition.

transcendental notion. The necessary precondition or the one attribute/characteristic that is common to all things.

BIBLIOGRAPHY

Agostini, Igor. "Descartes's Proofs of God and the Crisis of Thomas Aquinas's Five Ways in Early Modern Thomism: Scholastic and Cartesian Debates." *Harvard Theological Review* 108, 2 (2015): 235–62.

Anderson, James F. *Reflections on the Analogy of Being*. The Hague: Martinus Nijhoff, 1967.

Ankerberg, John. "Secular Humanism." *The John Ankerberg Show*. Complete Program Transcripts. Chattanooga, TN: John Ankerberg Evangelistic Ministries, 1986.

Aquinas, Thomas. *Commentary on the Gospel of John: Chapters 1–21*. Translated by Fabian R. Larcher and James A. Weishiepl. Washington, DC: Catholic University Press of America, 2010.

———. *Commentary on the Posterior Analytics of Aristotle*. Translated by Fabian R. Larcher. Albany, NY: Magi Books, 1970.

———. *An Exposition of the "On the Hebdomads" of Boethius*. Translated by Janice L. Schultz and Edward A. Synan. Washington, DC: Catholic University of America Press, 2001.

———. "On Being and Essence." In *Selected Writings of St. Thomas Aquinas*, translated with introductions and notes by Robert P. Goodwin, 33–70. Indianapolis: Bobbs-Merrill, 1965.

─────. *On Love and Charity: Readings from the Commentary on the Sentences of Peter Lombard.* Translated by Peter A. Kwasniewski, Thomas Bolin, and Joseph Bolin. Washington, DC: Catholic University of America Press, 2008.

─────. *The Summa Contra Gentiles of Saint Thomas Aquinas.* Translated by the English Dominican Fathers. 5 vols. London: Burns Oates & Washbourne, 1923–29.

─────. *Summa Contra Gentiles.* Translated with introduction and notes by Anton C. Pegis (book 1) et al. 4 vols. in 5. Notre Dame, IN: University of Notre Dame Press, 1975.

─────. *Summa Theologica.* Translated by Fathers of the English Dominican Province. Complete English edition. Bellingham, WA: Logos Research Systems, 2009.

Aristotle. *The Basic Works of Aristotle.* Edited by Richard McKeon. New York: Random House, 1968.

Bavinck, Herman. *Gereformeerde Dogmatiek.* 3 vols. Kampen: J. H. Kok, 1967.

─────. *Reformed Dogmatics.* Vol. 1, *Prolegomena.* Edited by John Bolt. Translated by John Vriend. Grand Rapids: Baker Academic, 2003.

─────. *Reformed Dogmatics.* Vol. 3, *Sin and Salvation in Christ.* Edited by John Bolt. Translated by John Vriend. Grand Rapids: Baker Academic, 2006.

Beaumont, Douglas M., ed. *Evangelical Exodus: Evangelical Seminarians and Their Paths to Rome.* San Francisco: Ignatius Press, 2016.

Damascene, John. "An Exact Exposition of the Orthodox Faith." In *St. Hilary of Poitiers, John of Damascus,* edited by Philip Schaff and Henry Wace, translated by S. D. F. Salmond. A Select Library of the Nicene and Post-Nicene Fathers of the Christian Church, Second Series, vol. 9. New York: Christian Literature Company, 1899.

Davies, Brian, and Eleonore Stump, eds. *The Oxford Handbook of Aquinas.* New York: Oxford University Press, 2012.

Davis, Stephen T. *God, Reason and Theistic Proofs.* Grand Rapids: Eerdmans, 1997.

Garrigou-Lagrange, Reginald. *The One God: A Commentary on the*

First Part of Saint Thomas' Theological Summa. CreateSpace Independent Publishing Platform, 2012.

Geisler, Norman. *Thomas Aquinas: An Evangelical Appraisal.* Eugene, OR: Wipf & Stock, 2003.

―――. *Christian Apologetics.* Grand Rapids: Baker Book House, 1976.

Gerson, Lloyd P., ed. *The Cambridge History of Philosophy in Late Antiquity.* 2 vols. Cambridge: Cambridge University Press, 2016.

Gilson, Étienne. *Elements of Christian Philosophy.* New York: Doubleday, 1959.

―――. *The Philosophy of St. Thomas Aquinas.* Edited by G. A. Erlington. New York: Dorset, 1971.

Hart, Charles A. *Thomistic Metaphysics: An Inquiry into the Act of Existing.* Englewood Cliffs, NJ: Prentice-Hall, 1959.

Hinlicky, Paul R. *Divine Simplicity: Christ the Crisis of Metaphysics.* Grand Rapids: Baker Academic, 2016.

Hodge, Charles. *An Exposition of the First Epistle to the Corinthians.* New York: Robert Carter & Brothers, 1857.

―――. *A Commentary on the Epistle to the Romans.* Grand Rapids: Louis Kregel, 1882.

Howard-Snyder, Daniel, and Paul K. Moser. *Divine Hiddenness: New Essays.* Cambridge: Cambridge University Press, 2002.

Hughes, Christopher. *On a Complex Theory of a Simple God: An Investigation in Aquinas' Philosophical Theology.* Ithaca, NY: Cornell University Press, 1989.

Immink, F. G. *Divine Simplicity.* Kampen: Kok, 1987.

Kennedy, Daniel. "St. Thomas Aquinas." In *The Catholic Encyclopedia,* vol. 14. New York: Robert Appleton Company, 1912.

Köstenberger, Andreas J. *John.* Baker Exegetical Commentary on the New Testament. Grand Rapids: Baker Academic, 2004.

Leftow, Brian. "Aquinas, Divine Simplicity and Divine Freedom." In *Metaphysics and God: Essays in Honor of Eleonore Stump,* edited by Kevin Timpe, 21–38. London: Routledge, 2009.

Levering, Matthew. *Proofs of God: Classical Arguments from Tertullian to Barth.* Grand Rapids: Baker Academic, 2016.

MacDonald, Scott. "Theory of Knowledge." In *The Cambridge Companion to Aquinas*, edited by Norman Kretzmann and Eleonore Stump, 160–95. Cambridge: Cambridge University Press, 1993.

Mayers, Ronald B. *Both/And: A Balanced Apologetic.* Chicago: Moody Press, 1984.

McInerny, Ralph M. *The Logic of Analogy: An Interpretation of St. Thomas.* The Hague: Martinus Nijhoff, 1961.

———. *Praeambula Fidei: Thomism and the God of the Philosophers.* Washington, DC: Catholic University of America Press, 2006.

Molina, Luis de. *On Divine Foreknowledge: Part IV of the Concordia.* Translated by Alfred J. Freddoso. Ithaca, NY: Cornell University Press, 1988.

Moo, Douglas J. *The Epistle to the Romans*, New International Commentary on the New Testament. Grand Rapids: Eerdmans, 1996.

Morris, Thomas V. "Problems with Divine Simplicity." In *Philosophy of Religion: A Guide and Anthology*, edited by Brian Davies, 545–48. Oxford: Oxford University Press, 2000.

Muller, Richard A. *Post-Reformation Reformed Dogmatics: The Rise and Development of Reformed Orthodoxy, ca. 1520 to ca. 1725.* 4 vols. Grand Rapids: Baker Academic, 2003.

Oliphint, K. Scott. "Aquinas: A Shaky Foundation." Nov. 7, 2012, https://www.thegospelcoalition.org/article/aquinas-a-shaky -foundation.

———. "Bavinck's Realism, the Logos Principle and *Sola Scriptura*." *Westminster Theological Journal* 72, 2 (2010): 359–90.

———. "Covenant Model." In *Four Views on Christianity and Philosophy*, edited by Paul M. Gould and Richard Brian Davis, 71–98. Grand Rapids: Zondervan, 2016.

———. *Covenantal Apologetics: Principles and Practice in Defense of Our Faith.* Wheaton, IL: Crossway, 2013.

———. "The Irrationality of Unbelief." In *Revelation and Reason: New Essays in Reformed Apologetics*, edited by K. Scott Oliphint and Lane G. Tipton, 59–73. Phillipsburg, NJ: P&R Publishing, 2007.

————. *Reasons for Faith: Philosophy in the Service of Theology.* Phillipsburg, NJ: P&R Publishing, 2006.

Ortlund, Gavin. "Divine Simplicity in Historical Perspective: Resourcing a Contemporary Discussion." *International Journal of Systematic Theology* 16, 4 (2014): 436–53.

Owen, John. *An Exposition of the Epistle to the Hebrews.* In *The Works of John Owen,* edited by W. H. Goold, vols. 18–24. Edinburgh: T. & T. Clark, 1862.

Owens, Joseph. *An Elementary Christian Metaphysics.* Milwaukee: Bruce, 1963.

Peterson, Michael L. *Philosophy of Religion: Selected Readings.* New York: Oxford University Press, 1996.

Phelan, G. B. *Saint Thomas and Analogy.* Milwaukee: Marquette University Press, 1941.

Plantinga, Alvin. "Does God Have a Nature?" In *The Analytic Theist: An Alvin Plantinga Reader,* edited by James F. Sennett, 225–57. Grand Rapids: Eerdmans, 1998.

Ridderbos, Herman. *The Gospel of John: A Theological Commentary.* Translated by John Vriend. Grand Rapids: Eerdmans, 1997.

Schellenberg, J. L. *Divine Hiddenness and Human Reason.* Ithaca, NY: Cornell University Press, 1993.

Sosa, Ernest. "The Raft and the Pyramid: Coherence versus Foundations in the Theory of Knowledge." In *Knowledge in Perspective: Selected Essays in Epistemology,* edited by Ernest Sosa, 165–91. Cambridge: Cambridge University Press, 1991.

Sproul, R. C., John H. Gerstner, and Arthur Lindsley. *Classical Apologetics.* Grand Rapids: Zondervan, 1984.

Stump, Eleonore. *Aquinas.* London: Routledge, 2003.

————. "God's Simplicity." In *The Oxford Handbook of Aquinas,* edited by Brian Davies and Eleonore Stump, 135–46. New York: Oxford University Press, 2012.

Swafford, Andrew Dean. *Nature and Grace: A New Approach to Thomistic Ressourcement.* Eugene, OR: Pickwick Publications, 2014.

Torrell, Jean-Pierre. "Life and Works." In *The Oxford Handbook of*

Aquinas, edited by Brian Davies and Eleonore Stump, 15–32. New York: Oxford University Press, 2012.

Van Til, Cornelius. *Christianity in Conflict.* 3 vols. Unpublished syllabus, 1962.

———. *Defense of the Faith.* 4th ed. Edited by K. Scott Oliphint. Phillipsburg, NJ: P&R Publishing, 2008.

———. "Nature and Scripture." In *The Infallible Word,* edited by N. B. Stonehouse and Paul Woolley, 263–301. Phillipsburg, NJ: Presbyterian and Reformed, 1978.

Vos, Geerhardus. *Biblical Theology, Old and New Testaments.* Grand Rapids: Eerdmans, 1948.

———. "The Doctrine of the Covenant in Reformed Theology." In *Redemptive History and Biblical Interpretation: The Shorter Writings of Geerhardus Vos,* edited by Richard B. Gaffin Jr., 234–67. Phillipsburg, NJ: Presbyterian and Reformed, 1980.

———. "The Range of the Logos Title in the Prologue to the Fourth Gospel." In *Redemptive History and Biblical Interpretation: The Shorter Writings of Geerhardus Vos,* edited by Richard B. Gaffin Jr., 59–90. Phillipsburg, NJ: Presbyterian and Reformed, 1980.

Recommended for Further Reading

There are too many books by and about Aquinas for anyone with a normal lifestyle to cover. The list below is highly selective, but does provide an adequate overview of Thomas and his work.

These two *Summas* will show the best and worst of Thomas:

Aquinas, Thomas. *The Summa Contra Gentiles of Saint Thomas Aquinas.* Translated by the English Dominican Fathers. 5 vols. London: Burns Oates and Washbourne, 1923–29.

———. *Summa Theologica.* Translated by Fathers of the English Dominican Province. Complete English edition. Bellingham, WA: Logos Research Systems, 2009.

It is useful for interested readers to read experts in the field in order to understand both the breadth of Thomas's work and the ambiguities that remain among Thomists. Good places to begin would be:

Davies, Brian, and Eleonore Stump, eds. *The Oxford Handbook of Aquinas*. New York: Oxford University Press, 2012.
Kretzmann, Norman, and Eleonore Stump, eds. *The Cambridge Companion to Aquinas*. Cambridge: Cambridge University Press, 1993.

See especially the biography of Aquinas as a helpful guide to his emphases and his overall approach. The best one-volume assessment of Aquinas is:

Stump, Eleonore. *Aquinas*. London: Routledge, 2003.

A good resource for the "new view" of Thomas is:

Gilson, Étienne. *The Christian Philosophy of St. Thomas Aquinas*. New York: Random House, 1956.

For a powerful critique of the new view as well as a call for traditional Thomism, see:

McInerny, Ralph. *Praeambula Fidei: Thomism and the God of the Philosophers*. Washington, DC: Catholic University of America Press, 2006.
Swafford, Andrew Dean. *Nature and Grace: A New Approach to Thomistic Ressourcement*. Eugene, OR: Pickwick Publications, 2014.

The best overall assessment and critique of Thomism can be found in:

Van Til, Cornelius. *Defense of the Faith.* 4th ed. Edited by K. Scott Oliphint. Phillipsburg, NJ: P&R Publishing, 2008.

———. "Nature and Scripture." In *The Infallible Word*, edited by N. B. Stonehouse and Paul Woolley, 263–301. Phillipsburg, NJ: Presbyterian and Reformed, 1978.

———. *The Protestant Doctrine of Scripture.* Phillipsburg, NJ: Presbyterian and Reformed, 1967.

———. *The Reformed Pastor and Modern Thought.* Phillipsburg, NJ: Presbyterian and Reformed, 1980, esp. chs. 2 and 5.

INDEX OF SCRIPTURE

INDEX OF SUBJECTS
AND NAMES

K. Scott Oliphint (PhD, Westminster Theological Seminary) is professor of apologetics and systematic theology at Westminster Theological Seminary in Philadelphia and has written numerous scholarly articles and books, including *Christianity and the Role of Philosophy* (Phillipsburg, NJ: P&R Publishing, 2013), *Should You Believe in God?* (Phillipsburg, NJ: P&R Publishing, 2013), *The Majesty of Mystery: Celebrating the Glory of an Incomprehensible God* (Bellingham, WA: Lexham Press, 2016), *Know Why You Believe* (Grand Rapids: Zondervan, 2017), and *Covenantal Apologetics* (Wheaton: Crossway, 2013). He is also the coeditor of the two-volume *Christian Apologetics Past and Present: A Primary Source Reader* (Wheaton: Crossway, 2011) and *Revelation and Reason: New Essays in Reformed Apologetics* (Phillipsburg, NJ: P&R Publishing, 2007).